MOSES led his people to the promised land . . . but *he* could not enter

GIDEON was offered a crown . . . that he could not accept

SAMSON became a weakling before he could conquer the Philistines

ESTHER denied her faith and married the pagan king before she could win the battle to save her people

WHO WERE THESE PEOPLE? Why were they chosen by God to fulfill a destiny they could not always understand . . . in a manner that often seemed less salvation than damnation? STRANGE HEROES presents their extraordinary stories, inspiring testimony to the transforming power of faith in the lives of all human beings.

Strange Heroes

David Allan Hubbard

TRUMPET BOOKS
PUBLISHED BY
A. J. HOLMAN COMPANY
DIVISION OF J. B. LIPPINCOTT COMPANY
PHILADELPHIA AND NEW YORK

Published by Pillar Books for A. J. Holman Company

Printed in the United States of America

ISBN: 0-87981-077-7

U.S. Library of Congress Cataloging in Publication Data

Hubbard, David Allan.
    Strange heroes.

    (Trumpet books)
1. Bible. O.T.—Biography. I. Title.
BS571.H74   221.9′22 [B]   77-1899
ISBN: 0-87981-077-7

Table of Contents

Introduction 7

1. Abraham: Father of the Faithful
   Genesis 15:1–6 9

2. Jacob: Conquered Victor
   Genesis 28:10–15 17

3. Joseph: Humble Courtier
   Genesis 50:15–21 25

4. Moses: Meekest Man of All
   Exodus 3:1–6, 9, 10 33

5. Joshua: Conqueror Extraordinary
   Joshua 24:14–15 41

6. Deborah: Prophetess and Judge
   Judges 4:4–7 49

7. Gideon: Crafty General
   Judges 7:19–21 57

8. Samson: Mighty Weakling
   Judges 16:28–31 65

9. Ruth: Loyal Alien
   Ruth 1:16–18 73

10. Hannah: Grateful Mother
    I Samuel 1:12–18 81

11. Samuel: Prophet to Kings
    I Samuel 3:10–14 89

12. Saul: King Who Failed
    I Samuel 9:15–17 97

13. David: King After God's Heart
    II Samuel 7:12–16 105

14. Bathsheba: Queen Mother of Judah
   I Kings 1:15–20 113

15. Nathan: Prophet of Wisdom and Courage
   II Samuel 12:7–10 121

16. Solomon: King of the Golden Age
   I Kings 5:1–5 129

17. Jehoshaphat: King Who Trusted God
   II Chronicles 20:5–6, 10–12 137

18. Elijah: Prophet of the Great Covenant
   I Kings 18:36–40 145

19. Elisha: Prophet of Compassionate Power
   II Kings 4:32–37 153

20. Hezekiah: King of Zealous Obedience
   II Kings 18:1–6 161

21. Josiah: King of Courageous Reform
   II Kings 23:1–3 169

22. Zerubbabel: Statesman Extraordinary
   Ezra 3:8–11 177

23. Esther: Queen for a Time of Crisis
   Esther 4:13–16 185

24. Nehemiah: Administrator with a Vision
   Nehemiah 2:1–5 193

25. Ezra: Teacher of the Law of God
   Ezra 10:1–5 201

   Conclusion 208

Introduction

It took me years to get over some of the things I learned in Sunday school. Not that I would downgrade the entire experience, for its overall benefit has been overwhelming. But some of my early impressions have had to be corrected.

One of them is that the men and women whose stories dominate the Old Testament were figures larger than life. Almost superhuman, as my imagination pictured them—unflagging in faith, undaunted in courage, unyielding in dedication. They loomed tall over me in those third- and fourth-grade days and reminded me of what I could never be. Their virtues seemed angelic and their powers almost messianic.

"Dare to be a Daniel," went the song with which we seemed to open our Sunday school period about once a month, "dare to stand alone; dare to have a purpose firm; dare to make it known." I was too unsteady even to be myself in those years, let alone to brave fiery furnaces and dens of lions.

Such singing and teaching, in my case, had two not quite happy results: the people God used seemed far removed from my modest talents and meager faith; and the God who used the people was himself overshadowed by their piety and exploits.

Unlearning this has taken a little time. I have had to read the stories again to ask myself afresh what God is saying through them. The technique of putting the narratives in the first person, as though the biblical characters themselves were speaking, is part of this attempt.

Surely the focus of the great persons of the Old Testament is on their Lord who made a covenant with them. Could we but hear them speak, their conversations would ring with testimonies to his power and grace.

They would also speak as people of their times, products of their culture, children of their history. Those times—and that culture and history—I have tried to sketch

7

as part of the background against which the divine drama of salvation was enacted.

Whatever else their story makes plain, it is startlingly clear that they were people like us. We can feel their problems and emotions as our own. They were puzzled by God's demands and surprised by his grace. Some of them knew the heartbreak of childlessness, the anguish of guilt, the temptations of power, the frustrations of disappointment, the perils of disobedience, the expense of dedication. Theirs were very human stories. They were *strange heroes*.

But they were people *God* used. In a sense, they were unique. We shall not see their like again, because the chapters in the story of God's love that they wrote are complete. The path they trod has come to its destination in the deeds and words of Jesus Christ, who is the Way for all of us. Theirs was a high privilege and a heavy responsibility. They were at hand when God was working wonders in the life and history of his people. They heard words that few were privileged to hear; they witnessed events that history will not see again—a national covenant, an exodus, a revelation of divine law, the establishment of a monarchy in which God was the true King, the messages of prophets who were enabled to discern history's course.

Their story, then, is both our story and God's story. We do well to hear it again as the major actors in the cast that God himself recruited might tell it to us.

My thanks for typing these chapters go to Janet Johns and especially to my wife, Ruth. She encouraged me to take the risks entailed in delving into the feelings of these biblical stalwarts and warned me of the perils involved in trying to analyze the wondrous ways of God.

Chapter 1

Abraham:
Father of the Faithful

After these things the word of the LORD came to Abram in a vision, "Fear not, Abram, I am your shield; your reward shall be very great." But Abram said, "O Lord GOD, what wilt thou give me, for I continue childless, and the heir of my house is Eliezer of Damascus?" And Abram said, "Behold, thou hast given me no offspring; and a slave born in my house will be my heir." And behold the word of the LORD came to him, "This man shall not be your heir; your own son shall be your heir." And he brought him outside and said, "Look toward heaven, and number the stars, if you are able to number them." Then he said to him, "So shall your descendants be." And he believed the LORD; and he reckoned it to him as righteousness.

(Genesis 15:1–6.)

The price was exorbitant, but what could I do? Sarah was dead, at the age of 127. I had to give her a suitable burial. For decades she had been my faithful wife and loyal companion. From Ur in the land of Sumer, to Haran in northwest Mesopotamia, to Canaan and Egypt and back to Canaan, she had been by my side.

Desperately I begged the Hittites, who owned the land around Hebron, to sell me property for a burying place. As an immigrant dwelling in those parts who was prevented by custom from owning property, I had no choice but to pay a premium price for land. The cave of Machpelah was what I had my eye on. And Ephron, son of Zohar, finally consented to sell it. Four hundred shekels —you heard me right—four hundred shekels was his asking price.

At first, Ephron had made a pretense of giving me the property. When I had offered to pay for it, he had protested: "No, my lord, hear me; I give you the field, and I give you the cave that is in it; in the presence of the sons of my people I give it to you; bury your dead" (Genesis 23:11). An attractive offer this was, but I had turned it down.

Legal title was important to me. I wanted a place for my family and me to claim as our own. I wanted roots in my land, after the years—scores of them—of wandering. To borrow the burying place, to hold shaky title to the cave was not what I wanted.

So I paid the price. And so "the field of Ephron in Machpelah, which was to the east of Mamre, the field with the cave which was in it and all the trees that were in the field, throughout its whole area, was made over to [me] as a possession in the presence of the Hittites, before all who went in at the gate of [my] city" (Genesis 23:17–18). Then I buried Sarah.

As we gently laid her well-wrapped body in the cave, my son Isaac and I, the warm winds of memory wafted across my mind. The memory of a call that came to me in Haran and sent me west to lands my ancestors had never known; the memory of struggle with my nephew Lot, whose selfishness and foolishness caused me pain; the memory of waiting for the birth of Isaac after Sarah's long years of barrenness—these memories swirled through my consciousness and reminded me of all the ways in which my God had tested my faith in him.

Tests of faith—one after another God sent them to me. And each time, in ways that I scarcely understand, he gave me strength to meet the test.

Take, for instance, that call I mentioned. When it happened, I was in Haran with my wife, Sarah, and my nephew, Lot. My father Terah had just died. Suddenly, without preparation or explanation, God began to speak to me. His presence was as real, his message was as clear as a conversation between intimate friends.

How different I found his voice from the chanting of the priests at the great temple of the moon god Sin, which was the central place of worship in Haran. His words were no cryptic code, no mysterious oracle that only a wizard could unravel.

His meaning was plain—too plain, in fact. It called for incredible changes in my life: "Go from your country and your kindred and your father's house to the land that I will show you. And I will make of you a great nation, and I will bless you, and make your name great, so that you will be a blessing. I will bless those who bless you, and him who curses you I will curse; and by you all the families of the earth shall bless themselves" (Genesis 12:1-3).

You can imagine the turmoil stirred in my heart at those words. I was to leave Haran just when my family had begun to sink its roots after we resettled from Ur, our original home in the south. I was to leave the tribe to which I belonged and the clan that I loved for a land whose name I did not know. Far from familiar sights I was to wander; in the midst of strange people I was to dwell. And all of this because of a call from a god of whom my ancestors and my kinsmen were ignorant.

What was it that made me respond? Why did I trust the words of this god who had thrust himself upon me? I suppose it was because he left me no choice. The power of his presence and the commanding character of his call were overwhelming. He simply moved into my life and took charge.

And then there was the promise that went with the call. The talk of becoming a great nation and having a great name was baffling, especially since Sarah and I had no children. But that voice and those words somehow filled me with confidence, and I found myself believing what I did not fully understand.

So we moved south and west, Sarah, Lot, and I. In a caravan we moved, our donkeys laden with goods, our servants pitching our tents and preparing our food. Weary of travel, scorched by the sun, anxious about the future, we arrived at a place called Shechem in the land of Canaan. There, as unexpectedly as when he first called me, God appeared and spoke again. "To your descendants I will give this land" (Genesis 12:7) was what he said.

I looked around me at the rolling hills, the rough shrubbery, the gentle valleys. Beyond the hills to the west lay the great sea that I had heard about but had never seen. Land for grazing flocks, land for growing crops, land for raising children, land for praising God—*our* land I was looking at, hearing but scarcely daring to believe. Again, the voice was firm; again, the word was clear. God had spoken, and I believed.

A nation, a name, a land—these were the substance of God's promises. What I did not know was all the struggle that lay between the promise and the fulfillment. The struggle with Lot, for instance. The details are too painful to expand upon. But some of them did flash through my mind as Isaac and I tenderly laid Sarah's body in the cave of Machpelah.

My thoughts fled back to that time when sharp strife arose between Lot's herdsmen and mine. God had blessed us both to the point that our flocks crowded each other for grazing space. I was tempted to rebuke Lot and send him to another part of the land, but something restrained me. Perhaps it was my recognition of all that God had done, my awareness of the grace with which he had blessed my life. I found it hard to be selfish when I really stopped to think about these things.

Instead of scolding Lot, I gave him his choice of the land. The Jordan valley was what he chose, lush, green, fertile, like the best fields of Egypt enriched by the topsoil of the Nile in flood. As for me, I stayed in the hill country, where my cattle had hard foraging and my herdsmen rough going.

It was the price of peace. And it was worth it. It proved worth it for another reason as well. Lot's choice put him in close contact with the city of Sodom, a contact which cost him nearly everything he had. Sodom's reputation was widespread, and a sorry reputation it was. Despicable sexual practices, men with men, were the custom of the Sodomites. As reports later reached me that Lot had actually moved to Sodom, I was filled with fear for his fate—fear both that he would take up their unspeakable ways and that he would share the judgment that was bound to come.

Once I had to rescue Lot from a coalition of eastern kings who had swooped down on Sodom and looted the city of its wealth and population. Clear to Damascus and beyond I pursued those kings with my servants and herdsmen, 318 in number. By surprising them at night we were able to release Lot, his family, and his goods. Still he did not learn his lesson. He returned to Sodom, and there he settled until the final judgment was announced.

Angels did the announcing, special messengers from God. First to me and then to Lot they came. The city was not to be spared. I had argued about this with the Lord and his messengers, but judgment was inevitable. Lot and his daughters escaped by heeding the warning. But Lot's wife was too attached to the city to turn her back on it and was struck dead by the hand of God.

Those tests seemed far behind me now—my call to a strange land, my disappointment with my nephew, Lot. As Isaac and I stood silently in the dim light of the cave and spent our last moments with Sarah's still, peaceful form, I put my arm on my son's shoulder and thought about the greatest test of all. As I did, I could almost hear Sarah laughing as she had done when the Lord and his messengers notified me that she would have a son the next spring. Ninety years old, she knew that she was well past the age of childbearing. Besides, she had never conceived a child while she was young. What hope was there for her now? So she laughed. Outside the door of our tent she laughed.

As for me, I did not know whether to laugh or cry. Twenty-five years had passed since that day in Haran when God had first promised me a nation and a name. Twice I had taken steps to help him fulfill that promise. Both times I was rebuked for my efforts.

The first time I had tried to follow the old Mesopotamian custom of adopting my servant, Eliezer of Damascus, as my son. The laws both in Ur and Haran provided for this. I would have taken solemn oath to treat Eliezer as my son and heir by saying to him in the presence of witnesses, "You are my son; today I have begotten you." That adoption ritual would have given him full rights of name and inheritance. But the Lord said, "No." We—Sarah and I—were yet to have our own son. I can still hear the words he uttered as he took me outside my tent: "Look toward heaven, and number the stars, if you are able to number them. . . . So shall your descendants be" (Genesis 15:5).

Once again I found my heart filled with faith. That same compelling presence that had led me from Haran to a new land overwhelmed me again. And I believed. As I did, I seemed to enter a whole new relationship with God, an intimacy which left me fresh, clean, new—like a baby just born.

Then the Lord startled me further by ratifying his promise in a special ceremony. Without going into all the details, let me say that he commanded me to slay some animals, cut them in half, and lay the halves side by side with a path between. I had seen this ritual before. It was a standard way to confirm a covenant between two kings. Together they would walk the path and take an oath like this: "May I be killed like these animals if I fail to keep my part of the contract." What surprised me most was that God put me in a deep sleep and walked the path between the slaughtered animals by himself. In other words, he took the full weight of the covenant on himself. It became his obligation to fulfill it.

Despite this dramatic ritual and its graphic lesson, I tried to help God once again, so desperate was I for a son and so doubtful that Sarah could bear him. With Sarah's encouragement I took her maidservant, Hagar, and had a son by her. According to the laws of our people, this son, whom we would call Ishmael, was really Sarah's. What belonged to her slave girl by law belonged to Sarah. But Hagar became too proud and insolent for Sarah to put up with, and we had to send her away before the child was even born. It was after this that the messengers promised Sarah a son in the spring and provoked her to laughter.

She remembered that episode when Isaac was born. His very name shows that—Isaac means "laughter": "God has made laughter for me," Sarah said. "Every one who hears will laugh over me" (Genesis 21:6). The laugh of skepticism had become the laugh of rejoicing.

And laugh we did over Isaac, and *with* him as the years passed. I surveyed those years as we stood together in the cave, until one memory stood sharper than all the rest. It was a memory that had no laughter to it.

It was another memory of that compelling voice: "Take your son, your only son Isaac, whom you love, and go to the land of Moriah, and offer him there as a burnt offering. . . ." (Genesis 22:2). My heart sank again as I thought about it: the wood, the donkey, the two servants, the three-day journey, the knife, the lad. But then I could hear that voice ringing with other, better words: "Do not lay your hand on the lad or do anything to him; for now I know that you fear God, seeing you have not withheld your son, your only son, from me" (Genesis 22:12).

Tests of faith? I guess I have had my share of them. But with what rewards! I do not know all that the future holds. I am old and full of days. Soon Isaac will lay me in this cave beside Sarah. But what more can I ask? I have my son and will soon seek a wife for him. God's promise has held good. Even this cave of Machpelah and the field around it are fulfillments of the promise. From the door of the cave my eyes scan the land that one day will belong to my family.

My prayer is that they, with me, will learn the lessons of faith. My hope is that they, with me, will serve the God who is faithful.

Chapter 2

———

Jacob:
Conquered Victor

Jacob left Beer-sheba, and went toward Haran. And he came to a certain place, and stayed there that night, because the sun had set. Taking one of the stones of the place, he put it under his head and lay down in that place to sleep. And he dreamed that there was a ladder set up on the earth, and the top of it reached to heaven; and behold, the angels of God were ascending and descending on it! And behold, the LORD stood above it and said, "I am the LORD, the God of Abraham your father and the God of Isaac; the land on which you lie I will give to you and to your descendants; and your descendants shall be like the dust of the earth, and you shall spread abroad to the west and to the east and to the north and to the south; and by you and your descendants shall all the families of the earth bless themselves." (Genesis 28:10–15.)

It was more than I could have hoped for. It was the reassurance that I needed. As he had done before, God met me at a junction of my life and affirmed his promises.

It was at Beersheba in southern Canaan. We were on our way to Egypt, my eleven sons and their children, sixty-seven of us in all, not counting my sons' wives. The journey was more comfortable than some I had made, thanks to the wagons, donkeys, and supplies which the Pharaoh had sent from Egypt. They eased the burden of my old age and gave me some protection from the infirmities of my 130 years.

Two things were weighing on my heart as we bumped along the desert road toward the oasis at Beersheba. Would I live to see again my beloved son Joseph, first-born of Rachel for whose hand in marriage I had labored fourteen years? And what about Canaan? Would my family ever return to its hills and valleys, to the land of my birth, to the land promised my grandfather Abraham and my father Isaac?

This was no casual trip to Egypt. It was a matter of life and death. Joseph, now a high official in Pharaoh's court, had predicted seven straight years of famine—five of them yet to come. Egypt was our only hope. Joseph's policy of storing grain during the seven years of abundance that preceded the famine meant sufficient food for all of us to stave off starvation. That was why we had pulled up our stakes, packed all our goods, collected our sheep and goats, and set out for Egypt.

As the wagon bounced and jostled, I was full of wonder. Would I survive the trip to behold the face of Joseph, gone from my side these many years? I had thought him dead, slain by a wild beast, his bloody coat the only remnant of the tragedy. And my other sons, would they settle in Egypt after my death and turn their backs on our promised home in Canaan?

At Beersheba my wondering was settled; my anxieties were put to rest. In visions of the night, I heard God's voice: "I am God, the God of your father; do not be afraid to go down to Egypt; for I will there make of you a great nation. I will go down with you to Egypt, and I will also bring you up again; and Joseph's hand shall close your eyes" (Genesis 46:3, 4).

Full of confidence, I headed south from Beersheba on the main highway that passed through the wilderness of

Shur and entered Egypt near Lake Timsah. There were many caravans plying that ancient route, none more joyous than mine. Some were carrying dyed goods and choice spices; some were hoping to barter hides for grain. But to me the grain of Egypt was secondary. I was going to look upon the face of Joseph. The other caravaneers would greet him as an overlord, chief administrator of the court of Pharaoh. I would embrace him as a son.

Part of a pattern in my life, this divine reassurance was. I mused on this through the long days of the journey. As we stopped to let the animals forage, I mused. As we plodded on, pursuing the setting sun, I mused. At times my sons and their sons wondered about my silence. When they peered at me puzzled, I just smiled. There was a lot to remember, and in those moments I preferred reminiscence to conversation.

My thoughts drifted to an earlier time when I had left Beersheba, pressing north and traveling alone. As I had watched the sun dip behind the western hills, the loneliness had closed in on me. With a stone for my pillow, I had stretched out to try to sleep. During that night I had the most vivid dream of my life. I saw a ladder—almost like a stairway—that reached from earth to heaven, with the angels of God moving up and down on it. Then the Lord himself appeared above the stairway and spoke to me in words of promise and encouragement.

I was overcome with the sense of his grace as he spoke. There I was, a fugitive, hurrying to escape the wrath of my brother, Esau, and my father, Isaac. At the urging of Rebekah, my mother, I had taken flight to go to Haran in the land of the Aramaeans, where I could find shelter with my uncle Laban. My mother's advice was based partly on her fear for my safety, and partly on her desire that I marry someone from her own clan rather than a Hittite woman from Canaan.

It was Esau that we most feared. And with good reason. We had just played a despicable trick on him. My mother had never been able to accept the fact that Esau, my twin, was her first-born. Actually, there was so little space between our births that I was born clutching at my brother's heel. My parents named me Jacob for that very reason—Jacob, "one who grabbed the heel"; Jacob, "one who tried to take his brother's place."

I was born grasping with ambition. I had lived the same

way. And my mother was ambitious for me. I was her favorite, and she coveted for me the inheritance that Esau deserved as the oldest son in our family.

Esau and I had always been as different as brothers could be. Esau was a skillful hunter, at home in the wilds; I was more retiring and preferred to stay close to our tents. Even our appearance was different: he was hairy, almost like an animal; I was smooth of skin. Our father took Esau as his favorite; he had an appetite for Esau's wild game. Our mother felt closer to me, because I worked with her a great deal in the chores of our household.

All this was background for the plot we cooked up to deceive my father and cheat my brother. This is a hard story to tell—and painful. The very recounting of it floods my soul with remorse. But tell it I must, because without it you will not know what the grace of God has meant in my life.

My rivalry with Esau came to a head *(birthright)* when our father was ready to give his final blessing to Esau. Weak and nearly blind, Isaac thought his time was short. He commanded Esau to go hunting and to prepare one last savory meal of the kind they had enjoyed together so often. Isaac would eat to the full and then bestow his blessing, in the Lord's name, on Esau.

My mother had other plans. She knew the power of such blessings and felt that God himself would stand behind any promises of prosperity that Isaac made to Esau. Her jealousy burned within her. She quickly cooked a meal of goat kids while Esau was out stalking his prey. Then she took part of the hide and wrapped it around my hands and neck so that I would feel hairy like my brother. Finally she clothed me in Esau's best cloak and sent me in to my father.

Time after time I had to lie to allay his suspicions. Covetousness, jealousy, ambition had squeezed every drop of decency from me as I stood before him. I reveled in the words of his blessing; it was all that I had craved and more:

> "May God give you of the dew of heaven,
> and of the fatness of the earth,
> and plenty of grain and wine.
> Let peoples serve you,
> and nations bow down to you.

Be lord over your brothers,
> and may your mother's sons bow
> down to you.
Cursed be every one who curses you,
> and blessed be every one who
> blesses you!" (Genesis 27:28–29)

My brother Esau was beside himself. Frustration pierced his heart like the arrow with which he hunted game. His spirit bubbled with anger like the caldron in which he cooked his spicy delicacies. My mother sensed how fierce his feelings were: "Behold, your brother Esau comforts himself by planning to kill you. Now therefore, my son, obey my voice; arise, flee to Laban my brother in Haran, and stay with him a while, until your brother's fury turns away" (Genesis 27:42–44).

Then came that dream and those words which have lodged in my memory like the roots of Lebanon's cedars: "I am the Lord, the God of Abraham your father and the God of Isaac; the land on which you lie I will give to you and to your descendants; and your descendants shall be like the dust of the earth, and you shall spread abroad to the west and to the east and to the north and to the south; and by you and your descendants shall all the families of the earth bless themselves. Behold, I am with you and will keep you wherever you go, and will bring you back to the land; for I will not leave you until I have done that of which I have spoken to you" (Genesis 28:13–15).

"Bethel," the very "house of God," I called the place (Genesis 28:19). That vision and those words found me lonely, guilty, fearful; they left me with comfort, hope, and courage.

In three days we would be in Egypt, my sons and I, in the land of Goshen, promised us as a legacy by Pharaoh. But Goshen was not to be our permanent dwelling place; Canaan was. The promise given to a fugitive those many years ago was yet to be fulfilled. The God who had made the promise had proved himself true. He had given me a fruitful family; he had remained with me in my wanderings; he had sustained me in my hardships; he had comforted me in my sorrows. I had no doubt that he would return us to our land.

Our caravan passed a company of Pharaoh's soldiers, marching east in search of bandits who harried the trade routes from time to time. Strong and disciplined they were, stepping smartly in their groups of ten. Their small shields of tough hide swayed with the rhythm of their march, and their bronze axes gleamed in the desert sun. I turned in my wagon to watch them until distance and dust shrouded them from my view.

And I thought of another army. After the vision at Bethel, I had reached the home of my uncle Laban, with whom I stayed for twenty years. Seven years I had served him as the price of his daughter's hand in marriage. Rachel was the daughter I wanted, but he tricked me into marrying Leah instead. And seven more years of labor were what I paid for Rachel. Fourteen years for two wives—fit retribution, I suppose, for my conspiracy against Isaac and Esau. And six years beyond the fourteen I had remained in Haran. Bountiful years those were, especially the last six. My wives and their two slaves had borne me children; even Rachel, for years barren, had brought forth Joseph, as an added blessing to my life; my flocks had thrived and multiplied.

In fact, my prosperity was more than Laban and his sons could tolerate, and jealousy became their response to my success. Hurriedly I gathered my family, my possessions, and my animals and moved west. Though Laban pursued us, I did not succumb to his pleas to return. Canaan was our land by divine promise, and it was time to go back.

It was on this homeward journey from Haran that I saw that other army. It was an army of the angels of God, sent to reassure me, charged with protecting us. Neither the jealousy of Laban, whom I had just left, nor the wrath of Esau, whom I was going to meet, could longer unnerve me. "This is God's army," I said as I gazed at those divine messengers (Genesis 32:1). "Mahanaim"—"armies"—was the name I gave that place.

The wagons rumbled along, swaying in the ruts of the desert road, and I was conscious of a pain in my hip. An almost chronic problem that pain had become, yet it too prompted memories of the encouragement God had brought in trying days.

My messengers had reported that Esau was on his way to meet me with a party of four hundred men. Quickly I gathered the animals that I had earmarked for a present to appease my brother. Goats, sheep, camels, asses, cattle —they were gathered, several hundred animals in all.

Then servants with droves of animals were sent ahead to meet Esau, servant by servant, drove by drove. My hope was that, when Esau and I finally met, he would have been thoroughly pleased by the chain of gifts I had offered him.

We were near the brook Jabbok when all this happened, east of Jordan and just a few days' journey from Bethel. That night after my family had settled for sleep, I went off by myself to ponder and pray. Suddenly, from nowhere, a man appeared and began to wrestle with me. Toughened by years of hard labor, I put up a strong fight and was on the way to winning when the man touched my thigh and put my hip out of joint.

Crippled, I knew I was in the presence of a being more than human, a being with the power to bless or curse. Instinctively I begged for his blessing. The blessing came in the form of a new name: "Your name shall no more be called Jacob," he announced to me, "but Israel, for you have striven with God and with men, and have prevailed" (Genesis 32:28).

When that hip aches, it serves as a reminder of that meeting with God, a meeting which enabled me to know firsthand the strength and power of God, a meeting which changed my name and my personality. "Peniel"—the "face of God"—was the best name I could think of for that meetingplace, where I had striven with God and lost, yet won.

The reunion with Esau was more than I could have dreamed. With a mixture of kisses and tears, we met. And in one embrace the grudges and the anxieties of two decades melted away. The God of protection, power, and grace had made it so.

God's steadiness despite my sin, his faithfulness in the face of my treachery—this has been the theme of my life. The ladder at Bethel, the army at Mahanaim, the wrestling at Peniel, the reassurance at Beersheba—God's presence was with me from beginning to end.

The wagons jostled, the wheels squeaked, the animals bleated, the children cried as the caravan edged toward Egypt. My spirit was at rest. The God of my fathers would go to Egypt with me. In fact, he was already there.

Chapter 3

Joseph:
Humble Courtier

When Joseph's brothers saw that their father was dead, they said, "It may be that Joseph will hate us and pay us back for all the evil which we did to him." So they sent a message to Joseph, saying, "Your father gave this command before he died, 'Say to Joseph, Forgive, I pray you, the transgression of your brothers and their sin, because they did evil to you.' And now, we pray you, forgive the transgression of the servants of the God of your father." Joseph wept when they spoke to him. His brothers also came and fell down before him, and said, "Behold, we are your servants." But Joseph said to them, "Fear not, for am I in the place of God? As for you, you meant evil against me; but God meant it for good; to bring it about that many people should be kept alive, as they are today. So do not fear; I will provide for you and your little ones." Thus he reassured them and comforted them.   (Genesis 50:15–21.)

It was more than I could stand. I slipped quietly behind one of the booths surrounding the marketplace and wept. After all my years of separation, after all my years of wondering, my brothers had bowed before me and brought me news of home.

My heart had leaped within me when I moved from the cluster of rough Hittites who were bargaining for grain to the group of ten men waiting their turn. Their clothes filled my mind with childhood memories and their language fell on my ears like a mother's lullaby. Then I saw their faces—rugged, tanned, wind-burnt, bearded, and yet familiar. Quickly I glanced from face to face, my heart scarcely daring to believe what my eyes saw. My brothers! My ten brothers, all but Benjamin, bowing before me in the land of Egypt.

I stiffened myself like a spear in order to retain my composure. Everything within me cried out to flood them with an embrace, to shower them with my tears of joy. But I restrained myself. There were some things I had to find out before I could make myself known to them.

They must have taken me to be an Egyptian. My Egyptian name, Zaphenath-paneah, my dress, my smooth-shaven face, my speech combined to confirm that impression. Through an interpreter I spoke to them gruffly: "You are spies, you have come to see the weakness of the land." Their protests told me part of what I wanted to know: "We, your servants, are twelve brothers, the sons of one man in the land of Canaan; and behold, the youngest is this day with our father, and one is no more" (Genesis 42:9, 13).

So Benjamin, my youngest brother, son of Rachel, my own mother, was yet alive. I was relieved. For years the fear had haunted me that the same jealousy that sent me to Egypt would lead my brothers to do harm to Benjamin. I had to see him, so I devised a scheme. My first plan was to keep nine of my brothers in custody and to send one to Canaan to fetch Benjamin. But on second thought that seemed too harsh an act. I feared that the shock of it would kill my father, Jacob. So I reversed the plan and decided to keep one hostage and send the other nine, who would also be able to carry supplies of grain adequate for the needs of Jacob and his household.

When I announced this plan to them, I learned something else I wanted to know. Because they thought that I was Egyptian, they felt free to speak Hebrew in my presence. "In truth we are guilty concerning our brother," they said to one another, "in that we saw the distress of his soul, when he besought us and we would not listen; therefore is this distress come upon us" (Genesis 42:21).

It was at that point that I had turned aside to weep. I took comfort in their remorse. They had acknowledged the evil of their jealousy and were willing to bear the judgment of the God of our fathers. As I wept, I pondered the mysteries of God's providence, the wonders of his protection.

The test of jealousy on the part of my brothers was the first of several that I had had to endure. And now I knew that, as in the other tests, God's providence had seen me through. As I wept, my thoughts fled back to that dreadful day when my brothers had turned against me.

They had taken our flocks north to Shechem, and my father had not seen them in weeks. Leaving our home in Hebron, near the place where Abraham our ancestor had been buried with his wife, Sarah, I set out for Shechem—a journey of three days. But at Shechem I found no trace of them or their livestock. Finally, after a lot of vain searching, a man informed me that they had moved a day's journey further north to Dothan.

From a distance I spotted them in the broad, green fields of Dothan. I ran to meet them, eager for reunion, unprepared for their angry reception. Instead of embracing me, they tackled me and threw me to the ground. Instead of greeting me with words of peace, they berated me because I had been my father's favorite. With vengeful spite they tore my coat from off my back, my coat with long sleeves which my father had given me as a special gift.

More than anything else, they kept shouting about my dreams. "See if those dreams of yours come true now," they mocked. "See if we, your elders, ever bow down in subservience to you, you dream-monger!" Then it dawned on me why their reaction was so violent. Some months before I had dreamed two extraordinary dreams. In one, my brothers and I were in the field together binding sheaves of grain. The sheaf I was binding stood upright, while their eleven sheaves bowed down to it. In the other dream, I saw the sun and the moon and eleven stars all bowing down to me.

My father was puzzled, but my brothers were furious when I recounted the dreams to them. Now, four days removed from our father's sight, they found their revenge. They were bent on seeing to it that neither they nor my father and mother would ever bow down to me in fulfillment of that hated dream.

They would have killed me on the spot had not Reuben intervened by suggesting that they drop me in a pit instead. It was Judah, however, who finally saved my life by persuading the others to sell me to a caravan of Ishmaelites carrying gum, balm, and myrrh to Egypt. Such caravans often carried young men and women to Egypt, where there was a ready market for household slaves.

Like lightning over the hills of Moab, these scenes flashed through my memory. More quickly than I can tell it, I relived that story and thanked God for his care. He had been with me through the shock of that hour and through the disappointment of the long days when I had meditated on the meaning of my brothers' anger.

Now there they were before me. They had bowed down to me. The dreams of my boyhood had proved to be prophecies, not fantasies. And more important, they had confessed the error of their ways. Reconciliation was possible—but not yet. It had to include my brother Benjamin and my father Jacob.

As I struggled to check the flow of my tears, other episodes sped across my mind, other episodes of God's providence in the midst of adversity. I thought of that day when I had fled, naked, from the room where Potiphar's wife had sought to seduce me. I knew her willful ways; I knew her wanton passion. I had no doubt that she would spare no effort to get even with me for refusing her urgent overtures of lust.

As I ran out of the room and left in her grasping hand my light tunic that I wore for work, I thought I was probably running to my death. In spurning her advances, I was saying farewell to the success and prosperity I had enjoyed as chief steward in Potiphar's household, where I had served since he bought me from the Ishmaelite traders in whose caravan I had come to Egypt. Now Potiphar's wrath was bound to fall on me. He had trusted me completely, and would be sorely wounded by what he would be told was my treachery.

Day after day that woman had been after me, first by subtle intimation and later by blatant invitation. Time after time I had explained my conviction to her, my conviction that to betray my master's trust and to enjoy his wife would be an offense against my God. Not that I was not tempted! She was an attractive woman, beautiful of face and form; I was a vigorous young man, full of desire. But it was not to be; my heart could not allow me to give in to my drives or her wiles. So I left my tunic and fled. And with that tunic, I left my hopes for success and perhaps for life itself. Or so I thought.

But God in his providence thought otherwise. Instead of death I got imprisonment. And, instead of menial labor in prison, I was placed in charge of all the other prisoners. The Lord was with me; and whatever I did, the Lord made it prosper (Genesis 39:23).

Like the test of jealousy, the *test of lust* had been used by God for his purposes, purposes which I did not always understand but had come to trust. Prison had confronted me with another test.

The story is too dreary to tell in full. But even a sketch of it will show how God's hand of providence had shaded my life from the scorching heat of adversity.

Two of the chief stewards in Pharaoh's household fell into disfavor and joined our group of prisoners—Pharaoh's head butler and head baker. One night they both had dreams which God gave me the power to interpret. The baker's dream predicted his death, while the butler's dream heralded his return to power. Deeply gratified by this good news, the chief butler promised to seek my release from prison as his payment of thanks.

Day after day became week after week, which became month after month of waiting. No word of favor was spoken on my behalf. The butler had forgotten. I faced the *test of neglect.* Never before had God taken so long to intervene, never before had blessing been so slow in coming.

Two years it took, and then the butler remembered. Actually, it took an urgent request from Pharaoh to goad his memory. The king had been deeply disturbed by two dreams which even his magicians could not interpret. Remorsefully, the butler recalled the help I had given him and told Pharaoh about me: "A young Hebrew was there with us, a servant of the captain of the guard; and when we told him, he interpreted our dreams to us, giving an interpretation to each man according to his dream. And as he interpreted to us, so it came to pass: I was restored to my office, and the baker was hanged" (Genesis 41:12–13).

That was all the evidence Pharaoh needed. He ordered my release and summoned me to the palace. As I shaved myself and changed my clothes, I rejoiced again in the wonder of God's care. From prison to palace God had lifted me. The test of neglect was over, and a period of fame had begun.

Pharaoh's dreams had to do with the cycle of the crops in Egypt. Seven lean cows had swallowed seven fat cows along the edge of the Nile in one dream. In the other, seven thin and blighted ears of grain devoured seven good and plump ears. God gave me the interpretation immediately: the land of Egypt was to enjoy seven years of abundant crops, fed by the regular rising of the Nile; then would come seven years of drought, when even the usually bountiful rains in the southern highlands would fail, and the Nile would be reduced to a trickle.

Then God gave me more than the interpretation. He gave me words of instruction for Pharaoh himself: "Now therefore let Pharaoh select a man discreet and wise, and set him over the land of Egypt. Let Pharaoh proceed to appoint overseers over the land, and take the fifth part of the produce of the land of Egypt during the seven plenteous years. And let them gather all the food of these good years that are coming, and lay up grain under the authority of Pharaoh for food in the cities, and let them keep it" (Genesis 41:33–35).

I was astonished at my own boldness in making these suggestions; I was more astonished when Pharaoh appointed me to carry them out.

From that day on, my life has been filled with excitement and satisfaction. The same God who had blessed me with these huge responsibilities had given me strength and wisdom to carry them out.

My eyes were dry by now, and my brothers were awaiting my permission to leave. Suddenly it struck me, as the rising sun strikes the great pyramids that shelter the remains of the ancient kings, that this too was a test—a *test of power.* How would I treat my brothers? What recompense would I ask for their jealousy and malice? Their necks were under my foot. I could break them or bless them as I willed.

They had done their best to do me harm, but God had turned their plans upside down to do me good. Would it be their attitude or his that shaped mine? Would I pattern my conduct on theirs or on his?

Those questions needed little pondering. I knew that grace and mercy were to season my deeds. I sent them on their way, with sacks full of grain and their money hidden in the sacks.

As they left, my eyes again flowed with tears. God, in his goodness, had taken me through all the tests—my brothers' jealousy, the woman's lust, the butler's neglect, the Pharaoh's power. Now that same God of all goodness would give me grace to wait for their return with Jacob and Benjamin. Our family would be together again. God —the God of my fathers—had so ordered it. And his will, his good will, would be done.

Chapter 4

Moses:
Meekest Man of All

Now Moses was keeping the flock of his father-in-law, Jethro, the priest of Midian; and he led his flock to the west side of the wilderness, and came to Horeb, the mountain of God. And the angel of the LORD appeared to him in a flame of fire out of the midst of a bush; and he looked, and lo, the bush was burning, yet it was not consumed. And Moses said, "I will turn aside and see this great sight, why the bush is not burnt." When the LORD saw that he turned aside to see, God called to him out of the bush, "Moses, Moses!" And he said, "Here am I." Then he said "Do not come near; put off your shoes from your feet, for the place on which you are standing is holy ground." And he said, "I am the God of your father, the God of Abraham, the God of Isaac, and the God of Jacob." And Moses hid his face, for he was afraid to look at God.

(Exodus 3:1–6, 9, 10.)

My eyes swept the horizon slowly from north to south and again from south to north. For more than half my life, it had been my deepest wish to see this land—the land promised to my fathers, Abraham, Isaac, and Jacob. A gentle rain and a fresh breeze had cleared the air of haze and dust, and all its contours lay fresh and bright before me.

As I gazed, my eyes paused to caress sites that I had heard of for years but had not seen until now: the dark mound of Mt. Carmel to the northwest; the harp-shaped lake to the north; the green tapestry of valley below me, through which the Jordan River wound its way like a brown thread; the Salt Sea to my left; beyond that, the bleached, rugged hills near Hebron which sheltered Abraham's tomb; and beyond all this to the far west, the deep blue of the Great Sea.

For a long time I looked at the new land. Look was all I could do. The people that I had led from Egypt and through Sinai were about to enter that land without me. My days had lengthened like evening shadows, and night was almost here. But for them—for those twelve tribes that came from Jacob's loins—a bright, new day was about to dawn. The Lord our God was about to settle them in the land through which our fathers had moved as sojourners. The great King was about to establish his kingdom among them.

I had thought of this as I had sung my final words of blessing to these tribes of mine, tribes that had caused me so much pain and toil, yet tribes that were the people of God, created by his love to do his pleasure. This is, the way my song had begun:

> "The Lord came from Sinai,
>   and dawned from Seir upon us;
>   he shone forth from Mout Paran,
> he came from the ten thousands of
>   holy ones,
>   with flaming fire at his right
>   hand.
> Yea, he loved his people;
>   all those consecrated to him were
>   in his hand;

so they followed in thy steps,
    receiving direction from thee,
when Moses commanded us a law,
    as a possession for the assembly
        of Jacob.
Thus the Lord became king in
        Jeshurun,
    when the heads of the people were
        gathered,
        all the tribes of Israel together."
            (Deuteronomy 33:2–5)

"Jeshurun" I had called Israel, as a reminder of the "up-rightness," the integrity, which was to be their way of life if they were to please the Lord their King.

The relationship between a king and his subjects was something that I knew a great deal about. My earliest memories are of a royal court; the first home I can recall was a palace; the companions of my boyhood were princes.

A strange beginning for a Hebrew? Of course it was, but a beginning in which the royal hand of God was at work. Egypt had just been through a wrenching change in rulership. A new dynasty had come to power that had very little sympathy for the foreign settlers who had come from Canaan and for centuries had lived and worked in the land of Goshen. The good will which earlier Pharaohs had shown to Joseph and his clan had vanished like dew under the noonday sun.

Fear mixed with envy in this Pharaoh's heart, and he took drastic steps to keep us Hebrews in line: "He said to his people, 'Behold, the people of Israel are too many and too mighty for us. Come, let us deal shrewdly with them, lest they multiply, and, if war befall us, they join our enemies and fight against us and escape from the land'" (Exodus 1:9–10).

Part of his shrewd dealing was to conscript our people for his massive building projects. As slave laborers we had to make bricks and lay them in place for the walls and buildings of whole cities. Another part of his plan—even more cruel—was to force the Hebrew midwives to kill our baby boys at birth.

My mother had circumvented Pharaoh's savage scheme by hiding me in the reeds near the edge of the river. Many times have I heard the Egyptian princess with whom I was raised—she was the daughter of a concubine in Pharaoh's harem—describe her surprise and pity as she discovered the floating cradle whose only crew was a Hebrew baby.

My first two or three years until the time I was weaned were spent in my own home, where I was nursed by my own mother. My sister, who had been stationed by the edge of the river to watch over me, had cleverly worked this out with Pharaoh's daughter.

From the day I was weaned until I became an adult, the Egyptian court was the context of my life. I became skilled in reading and writing. The sayings of the wise men I mastered. The standard skills of leadership I acquired. The hieroglyphics with which I wrote looked like those of any Egyptian courtier. In fact, I was Egyptian in virtually every way—dress, speech, manners.

But my heart was Hebrew. I found this out in a tragically painful way when I once came upon an Egyptian beating a Hebrew. I took justice into my own hands and smote the Egyptian dead on the spot.

Though I thought this deed of vengeance had gone unnoticed, somehow Pharaoh found out and put out a warrant against my life. I had no choice but to flee to the east where I could lose myself among the nomads who eked out a living from their wandering flocks of sheep and goats.

I found refuge among some Midianites who were also descendants of Abraham, through his concubine Keturah. There I married the daughter of Jethro the priest and resigned myself to a life of exile.

But then the King called. From the midst of a bush that burned but was not consumed, he called. With more authority than I had ever heard Pharaoh speak to a servant, he called: "I am the God of your father, the God of Abraham, the God of Isaac, and the God of Jacob. . . . And now, behold, the cry of the people of Israel has come to me, and I have seen the oppression with which the Egyptians oppress them. Come, I will send you to Pharaoh that you may bring forth my people, the sons of Israel, out of Egypt" (Exodus 3:6, 9–10).

My protests were in vain. The King had commanded and I went. I went despite my fear of Pharaoh's power; I went despite my questions as to whether my people would believe my story; I went despite my lack of confidence in my ability to be a spokesman. The Lord God, of whom I knew almost nothing, had appeared to me and revealed his saving purposes. And I went.

It was a powerful King who had called me. I knew that, because his call was irresistible. But I was to learn much more of his power in the days that followed.

With my brother Aaron I went to the court of Pharaoh. The ruler who had sought my life was dead by then, and a man I did not know occupied the throne. As I had expected, he rejected our plea that the people be released from their burdensome duties for a space of several days in order to offer special sacrifices in the desert. Instead, he added to the weight of their work by demanding that they furnish their own straw and yet produce their daily quota of bricks.

The battle was joined. The King of our people who had appeared to me and the king of Egypt before whom I had appeared faced each other in what would be awesome conflict. Plague after plague the great King sent. At first, the magicians of the lesser king were able to imitate the wonders worked by God. But then his full power began to show itself, and theirs was no match for his.

With blow after blow God smote the land. The waters turned to blood; the ground teemed with frogs; the air swarmed with gnats and flies; the cattle were stricken with disease and the people with boils; the land was pounded by hail, and the crops were ravaged by locusts; darkness thick enough to feel shrouded Egypt for days. But Pharaoh was unrelenting. During the pressure of one of these scourges he would promise to release the Hebrews, but as soon as the plague passed he showed himself as hard as the granite walls of his palace.

The final plague, however, was more than he or any human monarch could stand. Death stalked through the land and took the first-born child of every Egyptian family. More systematically than the Hittite army could have done, more thoroughly than the troops of Babylon, God marched through Egypt in judgment. The tribes of Israel were saved by blood, by the blood of a lamb sprinkled on the lintel and posts of their doorways, as God had instructed them: "The blood shall be a sign for you, upon the houses where you are; and when I see the blood, I will pass over you. . . ." (Exodus 12:13).

The power of our King—we saw it in those terrifying

plagues; we saw it in Pharaoh's grim agreement to let us go; we saw it in the crossing of the sea. God did not allow us to take the coastal road to Canaan through the territory of the Philistines. That was the shorter route. But the people would have been tempted to return to Egypt rather than fight their way past the Philistines.

Instead, God led us by the inland route to the edge of the Red Sea. There we seemed trapped. The marshy waters before us, the pursuing hosts of Pharaoh behind. Again our King showed his power. A mighty east wind parted the waters and dried the bottom and the Red Sea became a highway for our people. No sooner had we crossed than the wind abated and the waters returned to swamp some of Pharaoh's troops and to bar the rest from crossing. Free at last, we paused to sing of the power of our Lord:

"Who is like thee, O Lord, among
    the gods?
Who is like thee, majestic
    in holiness,
terrible in glorious deeds,
    doing wonders?" (Exodus 15:11)

In Egypt we had learned the power of our King. At Mt. Sinai we learned his demands. As I knelt speechless on the crest of that rugged mountain and heard the words of God, my thoughts bore me back to the courts of Egypt. I had often heard treaties discussed by the advisers to the crown. I had even read one or two myself. Of particular interest to us in those days were the treaties which the Hittite kings made with less powerful rulers whom they had rescued from attack by some common enemy. Vassal treaties, we called them. They recounted what the greater king had done for the vassal and what he expected in return. They were ratified by sacrifices and witnessed by the gods.

All this background of political contract, of solemn covenant between rescued and rescuer came to mind as the Lord spoke: "I am the Lord your God, who brought you out of the land of Egypt, out of the house of bondage. You shall have no other gods before me" (Exodus 20:2-3).

That was it! The King of the universe was making a treaty with the people whom he had saved. Our response to his rescue was to be total loyalty, full obedience. His laws stretched out to cover every area of our lives and to shield us from the foolishness and the wickedness of our pagan neighbors. With sacrifices and with oaths—but with no need for heathen gods as witnesses—we solemnized the treaty and pledged our allegiance to the Savior-God.

His provision for us from that time on was further proof of his kingship: the tabernacle and the sacrifices he provided as means of fellowship, even when we had sinned; the water, the manna, the quail he provided as means of nourishment, even when the people had complained; the cloud by day and the fire by night he provided as means of guidance, even in the worst of our wandering.

By grace and by judgment, he had brought us here to the hills of Moab, in sight of the land that was our legacy. Our weapons had prevailed against all enemies; our clothes had survived the rigors of forty years in the desert. His love had overcome the rebellion that delayed our entry into the land; his love had overcome my rashness that struck a rock when I should have spoken to it.

The King—the righteous judge—held me accountable for my angry act. My feet were not to touch the promised soil. But in his grace he favored me with this last long look at the land waiting for its rightful owners.

Filled with gratitude, I wound my way down the mountainside as the western sun splashed the sky with crimson. I would go to rest in peace. The King was in charge. He would see my people—his people—safely planted in their new land.

Chapter 5

Joshua:
Conqueror Extraordinary

"Now therefore fear the LORD, and serve him in sincerity and in faithfulness; put away the gods which your fathers served beyond the River, and in Egypt, and serve the LORD. And if you be unwilling to serve the LORD, choose this day whom you will serve, whether the gods your fathers served in the region beyond the River, or the gods of the Amorites in whose land you dwell; but as for me and my house, we will serve the LORD." (Joshua 24:14–15.)

The possibilities that lay before us were overwhelming. We could sow the new land with the seeds of our covenant faith. From beyond the Jordan to the Great Sea we could sow it, and from Laish in the north to Beersheba in the south.

I thought of this as the elders began to gather at Shechem. From all over the land they came, these comrades of mine, the heads of the families of Israel. My heart glowed like the evening sun as I looked into each familiar face. My spirit warmed like the desert wind as I embraced them one by one. My eyes were a fountain of tears as I recalled what we had been through together.

It would have been easy to become sentimental, especially here at Shechem, with its great well of memories from which to draw. Abraham had come here at the beginning, to the oak of Moreh. Here the Lord had appeared to him. Here he had received the assuring word after his lengthy and anxious journey from Haran: "To your descendants I will give this land" (Genesis 12:7). Here he had built his first place of worship in Canaan. Here Jacob had camped after his dramatic and peaceful reunion with Esau, his brother. Here Jacob, too, had built an altar to his God, the God of Israel. Here Jacob's ten sons had found pasture for their flocks when Jacob sent Joseph north from Hebron to seek their welfare.

This was holy ground, ground where our fathers had pitched their tents, met their God, built their altars. It would have been easy to speak in sentimental reminiscence here in Shechem.

And especially to this crowd, my comrades with whom I had journeyed for forty years in the desert while Moses was yet with us, my friends who had fought by my side against Sihon, king of the Amorites, and Og, king of Bashan. Now the smoke of those battles had long since been cleared by the warm east winds that waft their way from the brown hills of Ammon and Moab. The rubble of a score and more of cities had been raked aside and new cities had been built on their sites. The Canaanites, Hittites, Hivites, Perizzites, Girgashites, and Jebusites were all confined to small pockets, scattered throughout the land. Their proud cities were occupied by our people; their orchards and vineyards were growing our fruit; their fields were feeding our flocks.

Under such circumstances, in such a setting, with such an assembly, it would have been easy to become sentimental. But the overwhelming possibilities that lay before us were better watered by discipline than by sentiment. If our new land was to bear the wheat of our covenant faith and not the tares of idolatry, care had to be given to the dedication of the harvesters.

It was for this reason I had gathered the leaders of all the tribes, from Judah and Benjamin in the south to Naphtali in the north. Even the elders of Reuben, Gad, and the half-tribe of Manasseh, who had settled east of Jordan, were there.

Spirits were high as they gathered. The joy of old friendships, the delight of long associations, the memories of earlier struggles, the news of present successes bound us together with strong cords. Man after man reported the ways in which his clans were prospering. The "land of milk and honey" which had been our dream was now our reality. The generous bounty which Caleb and I had surveyed when we slipped into Canaan to spy out the land while Israel was still encamped in the wilderness of Paran —that bounty was now shared by all twelve tribes.

How thoroughly our God had fulfilled his promises. That was the thought that sounded strong in my heart like the blast of a ram's horn. How thoroughly God had fulfilled his promises!

I reflected on the way his call to leadership came to me: "Moses my servant is dead; now therefore arise, go over this Jordan, you and all this people, into the land which I am giving to them, to the people of Israel. Every place that the sole of your foot will tread upon I have given to you, as I promised to Moses. From the wilderness and this Lebanon as far as the great river, the river Euphrates, all the land of the Hittites to the Great Sea toward the going down of the sun shall be your territory. No man shall be able to stand before you all the days of your life; as I was with Moses, so I will be with you; I will not fail you or forsake you. . . . Be strong and of good courage; be not frightened, neither be dismayed, for the Lord your God is with you wherever you go" (Joshua 1:2-5, 9).

How thoroughly God had fulfilled those promises. "Every place that the sole of your foot will tread upon I have given to you. . . ." Those words had literally come true. My elders testified to that. The gentle lowlands of the south, sweeping down toward the coastal plain where the Philistines lived, were ours. So was the rugged Judean hill country, with its old towns like Hebron. The quiet valleys of Samaria were ours, and the massive mountains of the north like Tabor and Hermon.

Gifts of God those villages, those valleys, those mountains. God's every promise had been kept. "No man shall be able to stand before you all the days of your life." How firmly God had honored that word.

To my dying day one scene will be sharply carved into my memory—the collapse of Jericho's mighty walls. The whole experience at Jericho was an example of God's loyalty to his promise. No man could stand before us because God was with us.

When we arrived at the outskirts of Jericho I saw a man standing before me, sword in hand. Puzzled as to who he was, I asked him, "Are you for us, or for our adversaries?" His answer flooded my soul with confidence: "No; but as commander of the army of the Lord I have now come." I fell to the ground overawed, and the commander of the Lord's army said to me, "Put off your shoes from your feet; for the place where you stand is holy" (Joshua 5:13–15).

That sense of God's strong presence never left me. Jericho now seemed conquerable, despite its long history and its proud walls. But the method by which God chose to do the conquering was astounding. More than anything else, he wanted to teach us, his people, that the land was his gift, that our victories were his achievements. This was his strategy for battle: "See, I have given into your hand Jericho, with its king and mighty men of valor. You shall march around the city, all the men of war going around the city once. Thus shall you do for six days. And seven priests shall bear seven trumpets of rams' horns before the ark; and on the seventh day you shall march around the city seven times, the priests blowing the trumpets. And when they make a long blast with the ram's horn, as soon as you hear the sound of the trumpet, then all the people shall shout with a great shout; and the wall of the city will fall down flat, and the people shall go up every man straight before him" (Joshua 6:2–5).

We did what the Lord commanded, and the rest is history. To a letter, the words of our God came to pass. In victory after victory, no man could stand before us. In conquest after conquest, the ground on which our feet trod was given to us. Best of all, God did not fail me or forsake me. Wherever I went he was with me. How thoroughly our God had fulfilled his promises.

But with his promises came his demands. It was to make these demands clear that I had gathered the elders in Shechem. There was nothing new about these demands. God had made them plain to me when first he gave the promises: "Only be strong and very courageous, being careful to do according to all the law which Moses my servant commanded you; turn not from it to the right hand or to the left, that you may have good success wherever you go. This book of the law shall not depart out of your mouth, but you shall meditate on it day and night, that you may be careful to do according to all that is written in it. . . ." (Joshua 1:7-8).

How totally God expected our allegiance—that was the lesson I learned at the beginning. And I was reminded of that lesson many times along the way.

At Gilgal I was reminded of it. We had just crossed the Jordan—not by wading chest deep, not by log raft or rope bridge. We had just crossed the Jordan on dry ground. The Lord who had cut a passage through the Red Sea forty years before had now paved the way for us to enter the new land. Gilgal was our first campsite on the west bank of Jordan. There God commanded us to circumcise all our men, as a renewal of our covenant with him, as a mark of our total loyalty. As Abraham had been circumcised in response to God's promise, as Moses had circumcised his son on the way back to Egypt just before our exodus—so my men, the men of Israel, were now circumcised so that in all their living they would be reminded of how totally God expected their allegiance.

At Ai, as well as at Gilgal, I was reminded of God's expectations. The circumcision at Gilgal had been painful, but it was nothing compared to the judgment at Ai. For the first time, we lost a battle. The three thousand troops we sent against the city turned tail and ran. Like frightened lambs they fled; their hearts had melted and become as water. I could not fathom why they had lost their nerve, why a badly outnumbered foe was able to win the day.

Then God told me why. Someone among us had disobeyed his command at Jericho—his command not to loot, not to save any goods; his command to put the city to the torch, to offer it all as a burnt offering to him. It was a man of Judah who had violated the command, Achan by name. With broken hearts we punished him and his family. His greedy eyes had spotted a Babylonian garment and some gold and silver. Stealthily he had smuggled them into his tent and buried them under the goat-hair mat that served as a floor. His judgment was a terrifying way of reminding all of us that our God who had kept his promises bountifully also expected us to keep his commandments dutifully.

So here we were at Shechem, to be reminded again of what God expected of all of us. The great King had rescued us from harsh slavery and brought us to a free land. He had made a solemn treaty with us, a treaty in which he pledged his care and required our loyalty. For more than a century now this treaty had been the hope and guide of my life. Like the covenants that kings make with their allies, it gave me the assurance of God's care. Like the contracts that landowners make with their tenants describing their rights to water and forage, it told me my obligations to my Owner.

My farewell message to men who had marched through the land by my side was to be of this treaty. The King would have it so. Each generation needed to hear it. Each generation needed to reaffirm it.

The temptations were great—temptations to abandon our God in the despair of our failures, temptations to neglect God in the joy of our prosperity. Paganism was all around us. Heathen customs were steadily displayed before us. We had constantly to renew our pledge, to reaffirm our loyalty.

I reviewed our history: Abraham's call, Moses' rescue, our own conquest. I reminded these sturdy comrades of mine that all that they had, God had given. I urged them not to return to the false gods our ancestors had worshiped. I tried to set an example by my own pledge of allegiance: "As for me and my house, we will serve the Lord" (Joshua 24:15).

Their response fell on my ears more sweetly than a mother's touch, more welcome than a wife's caress: "The

Lord our God we will serve, and his voice we will obey" (Joshua 24:24).

Let God take me now when he will. My mission is complete. God has not only conquered the land; he has captured the hearts of his people.

Chapter 6

Deborah:
Prophetess and Judge

Now Deborah, a prophetess, and wife of Lappidoth, was judging Israel at that time. She used to sit under the palm of Deborah between Ramah and Bethel in the hill country of Ephraim; and the people of Israel came up to her for judgment. She sent and summoned Barak the son of Abinoam from Kedesh in Naphtali, and said to him, "The Lord, the God of Israel, commands you, 'Go, gather your men at Mount Tabor, taking ten thousand from the tribe of Naphtali and the tribe of Zebulun. And I will draw out Sisera, the general of Jabin's army, to meet you by the river Kishone with his chariots and his troops; and I will give him into your hand.'" (Judges 4:4–7.)

Singing was the only possible response to a victory that great.

"March on, my soul, with might," we sang, stirred by the sight of our victory over the Canaanite enemies (Judges 5:21).

> "The kings came, they fought;
> > then fought the kings of Canaan,
> at Taanach, by the waters of Megiddo;
> > they got no spoils of silver." (Judges 5:19)

Behind that simple stanza which celebrates our victory lies a long story—twenty years long, in fact. Joshua had been dead for many years. The tribes that he led into Canaan were scattered over the length and breadth of the land.

"Scattered" is the right word. Each tribe was preoccupied with is own problems. Herding sheep on nearly barren hills, clearing stones to plant vineyards, raising wheat and barley without enough rain, warding off marauding tribes —these were some of the harsh demands of life in those early years of settlement.

Only in emergencies did we rally to defend each other. Only on a few festive occasions did the leaders of the tribes convene for worship. Ours was a scattered existence. The common ties of our ancestry as sons and daughters of Abraham, Isaac, and Jacob and the ties of our covenant faith bound us together in a loose-knit confederacy, but our separate problems and the geographical barriers that crisscrossed the land made true unity almost impossible.

We had no single leader to whom we looked. Moses had come and gone; Joshua had joined him in the grave. No one had been appointed by God or elected by us to take their places. Occasionally when strong enemies mounted attacks against us, we would ask God for help. In such times he often appointed a leader—judges we called them —to mobilize the warriors among us and march them forth to battle.

Othniel was this kind of judge. For forty years God used him to keep peace in the land after the armies of Mesopotamia had continually ravaged the countryside.

But our people failed to learn their lesson. Again they

turned to strange gods and neglected the treaty that the
Lord God had made with them. That time it was Eglon,
king of Moab, that God used to punish his people.
Eighteen hard years the punishment continued, inflicted by
Eglon and his coalition of Edomites, Ammonites, and
Amalekites, our enemies east of Jordan.

Ehud was the judge God used to bring deliverance. And
after him, Shamgar won an impressive victory over the
Philistines.

So it went. An enemy would oppress us as an instru-
ment of God's judgment. We would turn to God from
idols and call upon his name. A judge would be raised
up to save us. God would grant him victory over our
enemies, and the land would enjoy respite from affliction
for a period of years. Then the tribes would grow careless
in their faith; they would compromise their loyalty to the
Lord of the exodus, and the cycle would begin again.

When Ehud died, we went through the beginning of one
of those cycles. This time the Lord gave us into the hands
of Jabin, king of Canaan, who reigned in Hazor, clear to
the north. Hazor was a magnificent Canaanite city which
Joshua had burned, but which our people had never
occupied. The Canaanites used it as a stronghold, and its
population came to number many thousands.

Just west of the Jordan between Lake Huleh and Lake
Chinnereth, Hazor's strategic location made it the base
for endless raids on the caravan trade between Damascus
and Israel and Egypt. For those twenty years I mentioned earlier, Jabin and his rough band of Canaanite
allies used their overpowering military might—including
nine hundred chariots of iron—to keep our northern tribes,
especially Naphtali, Zebulon, and Issachar, paralyzed with
fear like lambs before a lion.

As Barak put it in one section of our song,

> "In the days of Shamgar, son of Anath,
>   in the days of Jael, caravans ceased
>   and travelers kept to the byways.
> The peasantry ceased in Israel, they ceased
>   until you arose, Deborah,
>   arose as a mother in Israel." (Judges 5:6-7)

No caravan was safe, so persistent was the Canaanite
looting. No traveler could take the main roads, so oppres-

sive were Jabin's highwaymen. No peasant farmer could enjoy the fruit of his own labors, so pervasive were the marauders from Hazor, who rustled our sheep, raided our homes, ravaged our crops.

Why God called upon me to help, I do not know. I was a prophetess, not a general. My ministry was to help people with their personal problems, not to plot military strategy. But he *did* impress me with the need to act. The time of deliverance was at hand.

I sent a message to the town of Kedesh in the territory of Naphtali, some fifty miles north of my home in the hill country of Ephraim. In the message I summoned Barak to hurry south to confer with me. Four or five days later, when he had made the tedious journey, I delivered to Barak the orders which the Lord had given me. "The Lord, the God of Israel, commands you, 'Go, gather your men at Mount Tabor, taking ten thousand from the tribe of Naphtali and the tribe of Zebulon. And I will draw out Sisera, the general of Jabin's army, to meet you by the river Kishon with his chariots and his troops; and I will give him into your hand' " (Judges 4:6-7).

Barak seemed to sense the spiritual nature of the battle. With me, he knew that it was Israel's idolatry that caused the problem in the first place, and, with me, he knew that more than our untrained and poorly armed troops would be needed for victory. This, too, was part of our song:

"When new gods were chosen,
    then war was in the gates.
Was shield or spear to be seen
    among forty thousand in Israel?" (Judges 5:8)

Idolatry was the problem, and weaponry was not the answer. The power of God was. That was why Barak wanted me by his side. "If you will go with me, I will go; but if you will not go with me, I will not go," was the way he argued (Judges 4:8). He left me no choice. I packed a few things, and journeyed north with him.

From Zebulun and Naphtali, with later help from Ephraim, Benjamin, and Issachar, we mustered ten thousand men and assembled them into an army on the slopes of Mount Tabor. When reports of this reached Sisera, Jabin's general, he drove his army toward us.

It was here that God intervened in a mighty way. "Up!"

I cried to Barak. "For this is the day in which the Lord has given Sisera into your hand. Does not the Lord go out before you?" (Judges 4:14). It was not our equipment that won the day. It was not even the element of surprise as we swooped down the side of Mount Tabor to attack the enemy.

More than anything else it was the weather. God himself sent unseasonal rains and floods and turned the valley of Kishon, where Sisera's army had marched, into a stream bed through which the waters gushed in torrents. Sisera's nine hundred chariots, armed with iron and manned by a driver and archer, were helpless. The horses panicked; the chariots jostled each other as they were washed by the rushing streams; the foot soldiers were swamped before they could clamber up the sides of the valley. Sisera himself abandoned his struggling chariot and managed to escape on foot. The scene had all the drama of the exodus. And why should it not? The same God was at work, the God of whom we sang:

"Lord, when thou didst go forth
        from Seir,
    when thou didst march from the
        region of Edom,
the earth trembled,
    and the heavens dropped,
    yea, the clouds dropped water.

*   *   *   *   *   *

From heaven fought the stars,
    from their courses they fought
        against Sisera.
The torrent Kishon swept them away,
    the onrushing torrent, the
        torrent Kishon." (Judges 5:4, 20–21)

What power, what sovereignty! The very heavens, the stars themselves, the clouds were instruments of our salvation. God was with us; God was for us; the victory was ours.

But there is more to our story and our song. God not only used the elements as allies; he also used a person who was not even a member of our tribes. When Sisera fled that soaked battle scene, he sought a place to hide and rest. A Kenite woman, a member of a tribe that tried

to maintain peaceful relations with both Canaanites and
Israelites, offered him shelter and hospitality. With a sigh
of relief, Sisera settled in her tent, securely out of sight
of our troops. The rest of the story he never knew. But
Barak and I celebrated it in song:

> "Most blessed of women be Jael,
>   the wife of Heber the Kenite,
>   of tent-dwelling women most
>   blessed.
> He asked water and she gave him
>   milk,
>   she brought him curds in a lordly
>   bowl.
> She put her hand to the tent peg
>   and her right hand to the
>   workmen's mallet;
> she struck Sisera a blow,
>   she crushed his head,
>   she shattered and pierced his
>   temple.
> He sank, he fell,
>   he lay still at her feet;
> at her feet he sank, he fell;
>   where he sank, there he fell
>   dead." (Judges 5:24–27)

Sisera was dead, done in by a tent pin and mallet,
deftly wielded by a woman used to pitching tents. Sisera's
troops were put to the sword; not a man was left. The
Lord God of Israel had worked his will, and with unusual
help. A prophetess, a woman, had sounded the alarm and
summoned the troops to battle. An unexpected rain had
bogged down the enemy forces beyond help. A nomad
woman had assassinated the greatest general of our day.
And Israel was at rest.

We rejoiced, while Sisera's family vainly waited for him
to return. It was with the picture of that waiting that we
brought our song to a close, Barak and I:

> "Out of the window she peered,
>   the mother of Sisera gazed
>   through the lattice:

Why is his chariot so long in coming?
    Why tarry the hoofbeats of his
        chariots?
Her wisest ladies make answer,
    nay, she gives answer to herself,
Are they not finding and dividing
        the spoil?—
    A maiden or two for every man;
spoil of dyed stuffs for Sisera,
    spoil of dyed stuffs embroidered,
    two pieces of dyed work
        embroidered for my neck as spoil?"
        (Judges 5:28-30)

Singing was the only possible response to a victory that great. God's new deeds, God's strong deeds, called for a new, strong song. With that strong song came a strong wish, a wish that I, as a prophetess and counselor to my people, could share with all generations:

"So perish all thine enemies,
        O Lord!
    But thy friends be like the sun as
        he rises in his might." (Judges 5:31)

My strong wish is not so much that enemies will perish as that my people will always be God's friends.

Chapter 7

Gideon:
Crafty General

So Gideon and the hundred men who were with him came to the outskirts of the camp at the beginning of the middle watch, when they had just set the watch; and they blew the trumpets and smashed the jars that were in their hands. And the three companies blew the trumpets and broke the jars, holding in their left hands the torches, and in their right hands, the trumpets to blow; and they cried, "A sword for the LORD and for Gideon!" They stood every man in his place round about the camp, and all the army ran; they cried out and fled.　　　(Judges 7:19–21.)

I could not understand why they missed what shone so clearly to me. They wanted to make me king over all Israel. "Rule over us, you and your son and your grandson also," they had urged. "For you have delivered us out of the hand of Midian" (Judges 8:22).

A ruling dynasty they called for, like the families that governed the city-states of our Hittite neighbors. They wanted me and my family to mount a throne and wield a scepter like the Aramaean kings of Damascus.

My answer to their call was terse and pointed: "I will not rule over you, and my son will not rule over you; the Lord will rule over you" (Judges 8:23). I had to be blunt to deal with their grave misunderstanding. They could not have been more wrong, these beloved countrymen of mine, about the facts of our victory over Midian.

Certainly the Midianites had been routed. Certainly we were enjoying relief after seven cruel years of oppression. But to credit me for the victory was to miss the point completely. I almost blushed with embarrassment as I recalled how I had reacted when God first called me to lead the men of Israel against the forces of Midian.

That episode showed what a *patient* King our God is. Just before he called me, the Lord had sent a prophet to our people, warning us of the wicked ways into which we had fallen and reminding us of God's goodness in our past history. This was the gist of his message: "Thus says the Lord, the God of Israel: I led you up from Egypt, and brought you out of the house of bondage; and I delivered you from the hand of the Egyptians, and from the hand of all who oppressed you, and drove them out before you, and gave you their land; and I said to you, 'I am the Lord your God; you shall not pay reverence to the gods of the Amorites, in whose land you dwell.' But you have not given heed to my voice" (Judges 6:8–10).

Despite the prophet's words, I did not really understand why God had inflicted such cruel punishment on us at the hand of the Midianites. That is, I did not understand until the messenger of the Lord appeared to me. It was then I discovered how patient our God is.

I was beating the chaff out of the wheat at the wine press. It had been years since we were able to use the threshing floor, because the high mound and the open space which let it catch the fresh breezes to blow the chaff away made it vulnerable to our enemies. They would spot us threshing and promptly commandeer our grain. They had even stolen the threshing ox that used to tread our grain and turn our millstone to grind the barley and wheat into flour. Like vultures those Midianites would swoop down upon our towns and villages and plunder anything they could carry. Reports had it that their raids carried them to the edge of Gaza near the Great Sea in the territory of the Philistines.

From the deserts south and east of us they had come, across the fords of Jordan and into our homeland. Their tents dotted the hillsides; their flocks fed on our grain; their loot was carried away on our donkeys; they used our oxen to thresh our wheat for their bread. Seven years like the lean years in the days of Joseph we had suffered through, but without Joseph's silos full of grain. Lean, hard, hungry, fearful years those were.

I reminded the Lord's messenger of this when he visited me as I was threshing wheat in the trough where we usually pressed grapes, hoping I could hide our meager supply from the greedy eyes of Midian. Not only was I startled at the messenger's appearance, I was puzzled at his promise: "The Lord is with you, you mighty man of valor." My answer was clouded with doubt: "Pray, sir, if the Lord is with us, why then has all this befallen us? And where are all his wonderful deeds which our fathers recounted to us, saying, 'Did not the Lord bring us up from Egypt?' But now the Lord has cast us off, and given us into the hand of Midian" (Judges 6:12–13).

The Lord was patient with my doubt and persistent in his call: "Go in this might of yours and deliver Israel from the hand of Midian; do not I send you?" I was still not ready to respond. My doubts took another turn: "Pray, Lord, how can I deliver Israel? Behold, my clan is the weakest in Manasseh, and I am the least in my family." Again, the Lord was not to be put off: "But I will be with you, and you shall smite the Midianites as one man" (Judges 6:14–16).

My doubt remained stubbornly lodged in my heart like a boulder in a stream bed. The Lord's word had not been enough to persuade me; his promise had not been sufficient to encourage me. I tremble as I think back. The mighty King of our people had pledged his presence to me, and I was too dull to believe.

Brashly I begged for a sign to confirm that pledge: "If now I have found favor with thee, then show me a sign that it is thou who speakest with me" (Judges 6:17). Even as I asked for this sign I sensed that I was in the awesome presence of a distinguished guest, and I prepared a present for him, a present befitting his majesty—a lavish meal.

Considering our meager resources, the meal was a veritable banquet. A whole *ephah* of flour—that's a large basket—I used for cakes; and I cooked a young kid, one of the few that I had been able to hide from the Midianites. As I brought the meal to the Lord's messenger, he responded to my request for some sign to verify his identity: "Take the meat and the unleavened cakes, and put them on this rock, and pour the broth over them" (Judges 6:20). As I followed his orders, he touched the meat and cakes with the tip of his staff, and quicker than I can tell it a fire sprang up from the rock and burned up the food. While I stood staring at that sign, the messenger vanished from my sight.

The sign was enough. For the moment, at least, my doubts had fled. Yet I feared for my life. I had been in the presence of God himself: "Alas, O Lord God! For now I have seen the angel of the Lord face to face." With more patience than I dared hope for, the Lord replied, "Peace be to you; do not fear, you shall not die" (Judges 6:22–23). Like Abraham at Shechem, I built an altar to the God who had appeared to me. Like Jacob at Bethel, I renamed the place where the appearance had occurred. "The Lord is peace" I called it, a reminder of the well-being that I had experienced in the presence of God, a pointer to the well-being that our land was again to enjoy at his hand.

I had met the patient King, and my life was never to be the same. In the light of this meeting, I found the suggestion of my countrymen almost laughable. I, a king? Never! I knew who our real King was. And any competition with him was unthinkable.

He was a *jealous* King as well as a patient King. I found that out as soon as I responded to his call. His first command rang with his desire to be his people's only Lord: "Take your father's bull . . . and pull down the altar of Baal which your father has, and cut down the Asherah that is beside it; and build an altar to the Lord your God

. . . then take the . . . bull, and offer it as a burnt offering with the wood of the Asherah which you shall cut down" (Judges 6:25–26).

By night, with ten men at my side, I fulfilled that command. By night we did our work of desecration because our townsmen would have been inflamed by fear had they seen what we were doing. They depended on Baal for the fertility of their crops and flocks. A curious mixture their religious faith was. They had some memory of the wondrous deeds of the God of Abraham, Isaac, and Jacob. But they counted on Baal for day by day blessings, especially the blessings of harvest. Beside his altar was often erected a wooden pillar which represented the goddess Asherah, a consort of Baal, with whom he supposedly engaged in intercourse to guarantee the fertility of the land.

The sacred altar and the sacred pillar were both destroyed at the command of the jealous King. No rivals of any kind would he tolerate. In our day by day living as well as in our past history, it was *his* power that we were to celebrate.

Baal was no match for him. Baal's altar was leveled; Asherah's pillar was burned to ignite a sacrifice to the Lord. The God of Israel, the *powerful* King, had challenged Baal head on, and Baal could give no answer.

Despite this display of power, I somehow still needed further proof of God's ability and God's design to deliver us. I laid a sheepskin on the threshing floor and asked God to show his intent to deliver Israel by letting the wool be wet and the rock be dry when I arose in the morning. God met my test, but, to be sure, I asked him to *reverse* the test, which was even harder. He did. When I looked at the sheepskin the next morning the stone floor was wet with dew, yet the fleece was dry.

That settled it for me. If God was ready to save his people from oppression, I was ready to lead them in battle. I did all a commander should do: I recruited an army from all the northern tribes; I mustered them for battle opposite the camp of the Midianites. Thirty-two thousand strong, my countrymen came—the pride of Manasseh, of Asher, of Zebulon, of Naphtali.

God's next move took me by surprise as much as the original visit of his messenger the day I was beating wheat in the wine press. He ordered me to send back to their homes twenty-two thousand of my troops, who were fearful of battle. He made no secret of his reason: "The people with you are too many for me to give the Midianites into their hands, lest Israel vaunt themselves against me, saying, 'My own hand has delivered me' " (Judges 7:2).

The powerful King wanted us to know to whom the power truly belonged. Even ten thousand men were too many. God finally trimmed our number down to three hundred, who passed his test by drinking from a stream without wasting time in kneeling beside the water.

The rest is history, a history that will be recounted wherever God's people gather to remember his power. Like the plagues that smote Egypt, like the crossing of the Red Sea, like the tumbling of Jericho's wall, the story will be told.

The blasting of the trumpets, the flashing of the torches, the smashing of the jars—these eerie acts at midnight put the hosts of Midian in panic. Their army of camels, their strong weaponry, their arduous training did them no good. Like figs ripe for plucking, they fell into our hands. Three hundred men blessed by God decimated a mighty host. And God gave Israel rest from her enemies.

Somehow the men of Israel missed the point. They gave me credit for what God had done. They wanted to make me their permanent king. They wanted to set up a ruling dynasty in my family.

I knew better than to accept. Israel could have only one King. He had shown his patience when he called me to serve; he had shown his jealousy in the conflict with Baal; he had shown his power in the rout of Midian. I knew what he was like. I was willing to commit our future—and our lives—to him.

Chapter 8

Samson:
Mighty Weakling

Then Samson called to the LORD and said, "O Lord GOD, remember me, I pray thee, and strengthen me, I pray thee, only this once, O God, that I may be avenged upon the Philistines for one of my two eyes." And Samson grasped the two middle pillars upon which the house rested, and he leaned his weight upon them, his right hand on the one and his left hand on the other. And Samson said, "Let me die with the Philistines." Then he bowed with all his might; and the house fell upon the lords and upon all the people that were in it. So the dead whom he slew at his death were more than those whom he had slain during his life. Then his brothers and all his family came down and took him and brought him up and buried him between Zorah and Eshtaol in the tomb of Manoah his father. He had judged Israel twenty years.

(Judges 16:28–31.)

I should have fled as Joseph had. Even if it had cost me my cloak, I should have fled. But Delilah's charms proved too much for me, charms that promised such pleasure then but now have brought me to the point of death.

Her treachery has put me at the mercy of the Philistines. Her deceitfulness has shorn me of my strength. Her deception has robbed me of my eyesight. Her lies have cost me my freedom.

My enemies now make sport of me. Those hated intruders who continually harass our borders, who disturb our peace, who threaten our well-being, have taken great pleasure in my humiliation. "Call Samson," they cried in their drunken revelry, "that he may make sport for us" (Judges 16:25). To them my appearance in their great temple must seem a great triumph. For years they cringed in terror at my strength; now they have me wholly in their power.

To Dagon, their chief god, they gave the credit for their victory. Usually they held their great celebrations at the time of the grain harvest, for Dagon was a nature god to whom they looked for abundant crops.

I guess they thought that I was a bountiful harvest, after all the damage I had done to them through the years. I must have seemed like a bumper crop as they brought me in before the teeming crowds in the temple.

My eyeless sockets gaped in eerie emptiness. My head, so recently shaved, showed only a mat of stubble where seven handsome locks had once hung. My hands, which had once ripped a lion in half without any weapon, were bound with fetters of bronze. A battered hulk of a man, I stood, a tattered remnant of Israel's awesome judge.

One thought lodged in my mind like the head of a Philistine arrow: I must get revenge. That thought pierced me even more sharply as I heard the raucous voices of the hostile throng gloat over their victory: "Our god has given our enemy into our hand, the ravager of our country, who has slain many of us" (Judges 16:24).

Think of it. They were praising Dagon, the powerless idol, whom they foolishly honored, for my humiliation. I knew differently. I knew that the Lord God of Israel, the God of Abraham, Isaac, and Jacob, the God of Moses and Joshua, the God of Ehud and Shamgar, the God of Deborah and Barak, the God of Gideon took full responsibility for my plight. Not Dagon's triumph but God's judgment was the explanation of my collapse.

More than anything else as the deafening jeers of the jubilant Philistines thundered in my ears, I wanted them to know who the true God really is. If it took my life to teach them that lesson, the price was cheap enough.

If I had felt as strongly about God's honor and glory, if I had felt as strongly about my own integrity along the way, the whole story of my life might have been different. But regret and remorse could wait. I had yet some work to do.

Like a blind dog on a leash I was led by my guard out into the temple courtyard. I had seen the temple before, during my frequent visits to the land of the Philistines. Its architecture I remembered clearly, especially the two central pillars of wood supporting a roof that sheltered a portico. In the portico the distinguished guests assembled —noblemen, military leaders, heads of the great Philistine clans. On the roof were crowded the rest of the spectators. From the sounds of the mocking jeers, their brutal taunts, their fiendish laughter, I would judge that there were more than a thousand of them. My plan for revenge began to take shape. I hoped that in this dramatic moment the pattern of frustration which haunted my life would be broken. I prayed that my death would bring a success that had escaped me most of my days.

I thought, for instance, of an episode early in my life, when I fell in love with a Philistine girl. I had gone to Timnah, a village near my home in the territory settled by my tribe, which was Dan. Timnah was on the western frontier of our territory and had a great deal of contact with the Philistines, who lived near the coast. Sea people, the Philistines were. They had come from Crete and the other islands in the Great Sea and had settled on the coast. In times when our tribes were weak, especially in times when our faith in the God of Israel slackened and we did evil in his sight, the Philistines would penetrate our borders and plunder our goods.

I was born in just such a time. For years the Philistines had been chipping away at our territory, marauding our villages, stealing our women, capturing our children as slaves. Not that there was constant warfare. Most of the time the people of Israel were too weak to cope with the superior strength and weapons of our enemy. Besides, they were better organized, those Philistines. Their five great cities—Ekron, Ashdon, Ashkelon, Gath, and Gaza—were bound together in a tight political organization. Communication among these cities on the flat coastal plain was swift and simple. Our scattered tribes, consumed with scratching a living from the land, were no match for the massive political and military enterprise of the enemy.

All of this is background to explain what a Philistine family was doing in the Danite village of Timnah and why my parents did not want me to marry the daughter. Their protests I now understand clearly. Then, however, they fell on deaf ears: "Is there not a woman among the daughters of your kinsmen, or among all our people, that you must go to take a wife from the uncircumcised Philistines?" My answer was blunt, almost impolite: "Get her for me; for she pleases me well" (Judges 14:3).

Reluctantly they went to Timnah with me to meet the girl I thought I was in love with and to arrange the marriage. Reluctantly, I say, because my parents had high hopes for my future, hopes based on an extraordinary experience they went through before I was born.

The angel of the Lord appeared to my mother and gave her a promise about my birth: "For lo, you shall conceive and bear a son. No razor shall come upon his head, for the boy shall be a Nazirite to God from birth; and he shall begin to deliver Israel from the hand of the Philistines" (Judges 13:5).

I can imagine the conflict my parents felt. I, who was sent to begin God's plan for rescue, was about to marry a daughter of our foe. But God did not let me live with the bride.

I had posed a riddle to the guests at the marriage feast and had given them a whole week—the length of the feast—to solve it. They were thoroughly baffled and totally chagrined. They could not produce the answer. In desperation they put pressure on my bride, and she, in turn, used the power of her tears to loosen my tongue. Eager to enjoy her body, which had attracted me to her in the first place, I relented and told her the answer. I lost the contest, and I left my bride before I could enjoy the full pleasures of marriage. She had betrayed me into the hands of her countrymen. To gain revenge and to get the prizes I had

offered for the solving of the riddle, I marched south to
Ashkelon and killed thirty Philistines. Their garments I
left at Timnah as prizes. In hot anger and bitter frustration, I headed for home.

My frustration became even more bitter when I returned
to Timnah to claim my bride. Her father would not let
me near her. He had given her to the man who was best
man at our wedding!

Again my thoughts turned to revenge. It took some time,
but I captured a great number of foxes—three hundred in
all. I divided them into pairs and tied their tails together.
Into each knot I slipped a torch and released them in the
grain fields of the Philistines. The whole crop went up in
smoke before my eyes.

In encounter after encounter I had smitten these Philistine enemies who now took such delight in mocking me.
They did not mock when I slew a thousand of them using
only the jawbone of an ass for a weapon. They did not
mock when singlehandedly I plucked up the doors of the
city gate at Gaza and carried them all those miles to
Hebron. They did not mock when I snapped the seven
fresh bow strings with which Delilah, my new concubine,
had bound me. They did not mock when I broke the new
ropes that she had tied me with, broke them as a woman
breaks a thread.

Oh, that that kind of strength would return! Oh, that
once again I would feel that surge of power from the
Spirit of God. As a young boy I first felt it, as my mother
told me of the promises that preceded my birth, promises
that God would use me to begin his work of deliverance.
On the road to Timnah I felt it, when I slew the lion with
my bare hands. In my battles with the Philistines I felt it
—burning their crops, smiting their warriors, slaying their
mighty men.

More than anything else I wanted to feel that power
again. Not that I deserved any special favor from the God
of Israel. I had failed to fulfill my potential as a leader. I
had let lust and selfishness lure my steps into wayward
paths.

Yet somehow I had the boldness to ask for special
strength. I knew that my might came from him. I knew
that my long hair was merely a sign of my obedience to
him. So, shorn of my locks, robbed of my eyes, bereft of
my dignity, I called to the Lord in prayer: "O Lord God,

remember me, I pray thee, and strengthen me, I pray thee, only this once, O God, that I may be avenged upon the Philistines for one of my two eyes" (Judges 16:28).

With that prayer, I grasped the two central pillars that supported the roof and began to pull with all my might—or should I say, *his* might.

When I had been strong I had been weak—too weak to obey my parents when they urged me not to marry a Philistine; too weak to resist the weeping of my bride, who betrayed my riddle; too weak to turn from the charms of the harlot at Gaza, who allowed the Philistines to fall upon me; too weak to withstand the ploys of Delilah, who seduced me into sharing the secret of my strength and thus robbed me of it.

I had once puzzled others with a riddle. The honeycomb in the lion's carcass had prompted it:

> "Out of the eater came something to eat.
> Out of the strong came something sweet"
> > (Judges 14:14).

Now a more profound riddle came to mind:

> "Out of strength came weakness.
> Out of weakness came strength."

So it is with all who would truly serve the God of Israel. The strength of my life was marked by failure and frustration. The weakness of my death will be marked by success and satisfaction. The God of grace and glory makes it so.

Chapter 9

Ruth:
Loyal Alien

But Ruth said, "Entreat me not to leave you or to return from following you; for where you go I will go, and where you lodge I will lodge; your people shall be my people, and your God my God; where you die I will die, and there will I be buried. May the Lord do so to me and more also if even death parts me from you." And when Naomi saw that she was determined to go with her, she said no more.

(Ruth 1:16–18.)

It all happened so fast that I could scarcely believe it. It seemed just a short while ago that Naomi and I were making that lonely journey from Moab to Bethlehem. Our husbands were dead; we had no children or hope of children. Now here I was handing my newborn son to her.

Naomi beamed as she cradled my baby against her bosom. Her dark eyes flashed with joy as she peered into his ruddy face. With soft tones and special sounds that only grandmothers know she spoke to him as she rocked him gently in her arms.

Nothing could give me greater delight than this picture of my beloved mother-in-law completely at peace, supremely satisfied as she cuddled my baby. I had seen her in other days when peace and satisfaction were not her lot.

There were those bleak days in the land of Moab, for instance. I first met her about the time her husband died. Elimelech was his name. The two of them with their young sons, Mahlon and Chilion, had come to Moab in a time of famine. Freakish weather conditions had brought drought to the hill country in southern Judah, where their home had been. The wheat and barley crops on which they depended dried up in the soil. They had to move or starve. For some reason in those years rain and dew were more plentiful in Moab, so they had gathered their meager belongings, loaded them on a couple of donkeys and set out for Moab.

From Bethlehem they made their way north to the road that led east to Jericho. Then their route wound down through the barren, rocky hills to the great green valley of the Jordan. The oasis at Jericho with its ancient palms must have looked like the Garden of Eden to them as they slowly made their descent to the valley.

Then, with fresh supplies of dates, bread, and water, they crossed the Jordan just above the place where its mouth empties fresh water into the brackish water of the Salt Sea. Up the trail into the hills of Moab they pushed, before turning south to settle on one of our small plateaus.

Strangers—resident aliens—they were in our land, several days' journey from Judah. Our Moabite language was closely related to the Hebrew which was their mother tongue, so they were able to carry on their negotiations for water rights without undue difficulty, though in the ten years that they lived among us, Naomi and her sons never lost their Hebrew accent.

It was not the adjustment to a foreign land and its strange customs that made those days in Moab bleak for Naomi. It was the illness that plagued her family almost from the beginning.

We were near neighbors at the time. In fact, as a little girl I can remember that flurry of excitement in our clan when Naomi, Elimelech, and their boys settled near us. I thought it was strange that Naomi and the youngsters had to do most of the heavy work themselves, not only gathering wood for the fires and tending the flocks, but doing the plowing and cultivating as well. Elimelech spent most of his time in the tent, and when he did venture out it was only to walk a few steps around the campsite.

Finally it happened. I guess I was about twelve at the time. Early in the morning Mahlon and Chilion came running to our tents weeping, almost screaming. "Father is dead," they cried out in great sobs of shock and grief.

Bravely Naomi held her family together as they squeezed out their existence from the crops that our hardy hills grudgingly yielded. My family did what they could to help, and a strong bond of friendship developed between Naomi and my parents. It was almost inevitable that I would marry one of her sons. When my father announced to me that the arrangements for my marriage were all settled, my heart leaped for joy. Nothing could have pleased me more than to have Naomi as a mother-in-law. Her kindly spirit, her gentle voice, her courageous heart—all these had made a sharp impression on me as I was growing up. And there was something else—her strong faith in the God of Israel.

Often I had listened as she told Mahlon and Chilion about the great deeds of the God of Abraham, Isaac, and Jacob, the ancestors of the Hebrews. His power, his holiness, his love she spoke about in words of devotion and wonder. Never had I heard stories like those she told—a God who defeated the Egyptians, a God who dried up the Jordan, a God who conquered Jericho. Our Moabite god, Chemash, seemed to be of an entirely different sort—

fickle, whimsical, cruel. Sometimes he even required people to sacrifice their children to him. And besides that, he had no power outside of Moab. Naomi's God seemed to be powerful wherever his people were.

Our days of joy after the wedding feast were short-lived. The brightness that Naomi knew for a time as her family flourished with the love and companionship of two young daughters-in-law, Orpah and me, once again paled as illness struck. We tried everything we knew—the three of us—to bring healing to our men. We bathed their burning brows in olive oil; we wet their parched lips with goat's milk; we sat by their sides night and day, taking turns working, watching, sleeping. No balm brought healing, no prayer was answered.

What a dreary picture we must have made setting out from Moab on the journey to Judah—three widows, bereft of husbands, unblessed by children. What an emptiness Naomi must have felt. She had made the trip east just ten years before, high with hope, one woman with three men. Now she was shorn of husband and sons—no line, no heritage, and no hope of any.

With characteristic unselfishness she put our welfare—Orpah's and mine—ahead of her own. "Go, return each of you to her mother's house. May the Lord deal kindly with you, as you have dealt with the dead and with me. The Lord grant that you may find a home, each of you in the house of her husband!" (Ruth 1:8-9).

I was tempted to follow her advice. I had never been a day's journey from home before. A new land, a new culture—I was frightened at the thought. Yet was there really much more for me at home? My parents were aged; my family had scattered. Besides, what place would a widow have? No man wanted a used woman. I would only have been a burden—and an embarrassment—to my kinsmen.

We bade Orpah a tearful good-bye when she decided to turn back, and set our faces toward the west. We were not exuberant with joy—Naomi and I—but at least we had each other. "Entreat me not to leave you or to return from following you," I begged Naomi. "For where you go I will go, and where you lodge I will lodge; your people shall be my people, and your God my God; where you die I will die, and there will I be buried." Then with a sharp gesture as though I was slitting my throat, I took the

strongest possible oath: "May the Lord do so to me and
more also if even death parts me from you" (Ruth
1:16–17). Naomi's silence told me that she knew how determined I was. And the warmth that shone from her eyes
told me how grateful she was for my determination.

For the two of us just to survive was a struggle, so we
were glad that the barley harvest was in full sway when
we arrived at Bethlehem. It became my job to follow after
the harvesters to pick up the gleanings that they dropped,
and to cut the edges of the fields which they deliberately
left untouched. The laws and customs of Israel made special provision for this gleaning. Widows who had no family
to provide for them, and aliens who were not allowed to
purchase land for themselves, were given special permission to glean in the fields in order to keep bread on their
tables. *Compassion* was the explanation the Israelites gave
for this custom. Because their God had had compassion on
them when they were slaves in Egypt they were to have
compassion on others, especially widows, orphans, and
aliens. I qualified on two counts: I was a widow and an
alien. And they certainly showed compassion to me.

Especially Boaz, a wealthy landowner in whose field I
had gone to glean. He was a relative of Naomi's late husband, and we hoped he might show us special kindness.
He did—and beyond anything we could have hoped for.
He encouraged me to stay in his fields; he ordered the
young men not to molest me; he provided water for my
thirst. When I asked him, "Why all this kindness to a
stranger?", his reply delighted my spirit: "All that you
have done for your mother-in-law since the death of your
husband has been fully told me, and how you left your
father and mother and your native land and came to a
people that you did not know before. The Lord recompense you for what you have done, and a full reward be
given you by the Lord, the God of Israel, under whose
wings you have come to take refuge" (Ruth 2:11–12).

My tongue tripped over itself as I tried to tell Naomi
almost in one breath what Boaz had said and done. Day
after day, through the entire barley harvest, Boaz's acts
of kindness continued—protection, water, food, extra
sheaves of barley. Each evening as I brought home my
abundant supply of grain and recounted the gracious
deeds of Boaz, I could sense that Naomi was not only
listening, she was planning.

Finally, her plan came out. It was a scary plan. Naomi had to rehearse it with me step by step before I gained courage to carry it out. I was to go at night to the threshing floor where Boaz had been working and where he would spend the night. Bathed, perfumed, clothed in my best, I was to go to Boaz and lie at his feet.

Naomi's plan was not just to find me a husband. It was to find a man among the kinsmen of her husband and my husband who would take me as wife and help me raise up a son to carry on the family line. Without this, Elimelech's name would perish, and there would be no remembrance of him among the clans of Bethlehem.

It was this that I told Boaz when I awakened him by the threshing floor at midnight: "I am Ruth, your maidservant; spread your skirt over your maidservant, for you are next of kin" (Ruth 3:9). Boaz knew what I meant. As a close kinsman it was his duty to see that the family line was kept unbroken. The survival of the clans of Israel depended on the faithfulness of each kinsman to do his duty, when relatives had died childless.

Boaz was willing, perhaps eager. But there was a problem. He was not the *next* of kin. Someone else had even a closer relationship to Elimelech and therefore a greater responsibility to Naomi and me.

My heart was heavy with uncertainty as I waited for news from the city gate. There Boaz, with ten elders of the town as witnesses, was to discuss the matter with the nearer relative. The hours dragged by as we waited for the results of that meeting.

Finally Boaz's messenger summoned us, and we heard from Boaz himself the good news. The nearer relative had been willing to buy Naomi's land, which had been heavily mortgaged in the days of famine. Rightly, he refused to let the parcel which was part of the family heritage, apportioned to Elimelech's fathers in the days of Joshua, be sold outside the clan. But when the kinsman heard that he would have to marry me and support me, the deal had proved more than he could afford. And so he relinquished his rights to both field and wife to Boaz. Before the ten witnesses, in a legal transaction, he relinquished his rights. Boaz, my husband's kinsman, had become my redeemer.

No wonder Naomi beamed with joy as she held our baby. When we first arrived from Moab she had told the

women of Bethlehem not to call her Naomi, which means
"pleasant," but to call her Mara, or "bitter." Now she was
blessing the name of the God of Israel. "I went away full,"
she had said, "and the Lord has brought me back empty"
(Ruth 1:21). Now she was full again, and to her God—
to *our* God—she gave thanks. And so did I.

Chapter 10

Hannah:
Grateful Mother

As she continued praying before the LORD, Eli observed her mouth. Hannah was speaking in her heart; only her lips moved, and her voice was not heard; therefore Eli took her to be a drunken woman. And Eli said to her, "How long will you be drunken? Put away your wine from you." But Hannah answered, "No, my lord, I am a woman sorely troubled; I have drunk neither wine nor strong drink, but I have been pouring out my soul before the LORD. Do not regard your maidservant as a base woman, for all along I have been speaking out of my great anxiety and vexation." Then Eli answered, "Go in peace, and the God of Israel grant your petition which you have made to him." And she said, "Let your maidservant find favor in your eyes." Then the woman went her way and ate, and her countenance was no longer sad. (I Samuel 1:12–18.)

I could hardly wait to see Samuel again. My fingers fairly flew as they put the final stitches in his new robe. I held it up in front of me to make sure it was long enough. Last year when our family made the trip to Shiloh, he was almost as tall as I was. By this year he had probably grown another couple of inches. And the sleeves—had I allowed enough room for those long arms of his?

Nothing I did all year gave me more personal pleasure than making the robe. I would wait for the finest wool that I could find in the market at Ramah. Then I would spend all the time needed to card it and clean it. The spinning and weaving took a lot of time, but as each thread fell into place I knew I was closer to the hour when Elkanah and I would set out for Shiloh to see Samuel.

Samuel—his very name was music to my ears. And more than music, it was a reminder that God had heard my prayer. "The name of God" is what Samuel means, and behind that name is a remarkable story.

Stitching this robe reminded me of it. For how many years did I watch Peninnah, my husband's other wife, stitch garments for her children? For how many years did I suffer her scornful glances as she proudly clothed her children?

She looked at me as though I were cursed—Peninnah did. And sometimes I felt as though I were. Month after month I waited for signs that a child was on the way. And month after month I was painfully reminded of my barrenness.

Peninnah's pregnancies were almost more than I could endure. Her face glowed with satisfaction as her body grew in bulk. When she delivered her children, she became almost insufferable. In smug satisfaction she nursed her babies; with an air of superiority she changed their swaddling clothes.

Every lesson they learned, every step they took became opportunities for her to boast. And not only to boast, but to mock: "Why is it, Hannah, that God has not blessed your womb? What shameful deed are you hiding, what wicked words have you spoken, that God has cursed you so?"

Here I was planning with great anticipation for the trip

to Shiloh, scurrying to get ready, hurrying to finish Samuel's robe. I found myself laughing at my eagerness. It had certainly been different in the days when I was barren. I dreaded the trip then. I'm almost ashamed to admit it, but I dreaded the trip. Even though we were going to Shiloh to worship at the tabernacle, I dreaded it. Even though the great ark of the covenant was there that Moses had built in the desert and that Joshua's men had carried over Jordan on dry ground, I dreaded it. Even though it was a time of great reunion with loved ones and a time of great fellowship with the God of our fathers, I dreaded it.

I dreaded it because Elkanah always showed favor to Peninnah when we went to Shiloh. Not that he did not love me, but he was puzzled as to why God had closed my womb. When our turn came to eat the sacrificial feast, Elkanah would give extra portions to Peninnah and only a single portion to me. Apparently he thought she had been more blessed by God than I was, and so he showed her this special favor. He gave her the most to eat and from the choicest portion of the sacrificial animal—and all of this in public.

If Peninnah was difficult to live with in the privacy of our tents, she was unbearable in public. With mocking gestures she accepted her special portions; with haughty disdain she made loud remarks about my simple serving. My heart ached within me with double pain: I hated my rival and I yearned for a son.

Finally, once at Shiloh I lost all appetite even for the sacrificial meal, and my frustration gave way to tears that gushed from my eyes like the mountain streams in the spring rains.

Elkanah spoke to me: "Hannah, why do you weep? And why do you not eat? And why is your heart sad? Am I not more to you than ten sons?" (I Samuel 1:8). He did mean a lot to me. Elkanah was a splendid husband, more than I could have wished for. But no husband, no matter how noble and kind, could ease that aching in my womb, that soreness in my spirit. Only a son could do that.

In desperation I left our group and their celebration and went near the tabernacle to pray. Mustering courage almost to the point of recklessness, I lifted my request to our God. And I sealed that request with a vow: "O Lord of hosts, if thou wilt indeed look on the affliction of thy maidservant, and remember me, and not forget thy maid-

servant, but wilt give to thy maidservant a son, then I will
give him to the Lord all the days of his life, and no razor
shall touch his head" (I Samuel 1:11).

As I prayed I remembered how God had answered such
prayers before. I was begging him to do it again. "As you
gave Isaac to Sarah when she was well past the age of
bearing, so bless my womb with child that I may join in
Sarah's laughing. As you gave twins to barren Rebekah to
keep your promise to Abraham, so give me just one son
and I will give him back to you. As you honored Rachel's
prayer with the gift of our father Joseph and gladdened
the heart of Jacob, so lift the burden of my shame that I
may eat with joy the food of sacrifice. As you began the
work of deliverance from Philistine oppression by spark-
ing life in the barren body of Manoah's wife, so show your
saving power in me."

My burden of prayer was too deep to be expressed
aloud. Silently I sent these petitions heavenward, barely
moving my lips to frame my thoughts. Suddenly I was
aware of a figure beside me. It was Eli, the priest of
Shiloh. I recognized him; he did not recognize me. "How
long will you be drunken?" he rebuked me. "Put away
your wine from you." Shocked at his words, I raised my
protest: "No, my lord, I am a woman sorely troubled; I
have drunk neither wine nor strong drink, but I have been
pouring out my soul before the Lord. Do not regard your
maidservant as a base woman, for all along I have been
speaking out of my great anxiety and vexation." His response changed my whole life: "Go in peace, and the God
of Israel grant your petition which you have made to him"
(I Samuel 1:14–17).

The next year I did not go to Shiloh. I was nursing my
son Samuel. God had heard my prayer; the blessing of Eli
had come true. For a couple of years I stayed home, in
fact. Then, finally, Samuel was weaned. He was nearly
three by then, a healthy, round-faced child. Since he could
understand anything at all, I had told him the story of his
birth—and of my vow.

Then the time came to fulfill it, and off to Shiloh we
went. With food for the two-day journey there and back,
we went. With a bull for our sacrifice, with meal and wine
for our offerings, we went. And with a year's supply of
clothes for Samuel, whom we would leave in Shiloh, we
went.

I suppose I argued some with myself over that vow. Did I have to keep it? Was there another way to keep it? But I always lost such arguments. I had offered my son to God before his conception; I could not withdraw that offer now.

Elkanah and I slew our sacrifice and then brought Samuel to Eli. "Oh, my lord! As you live, my lord, I am the woman who was standing here in your presence, praying to the Lord. For this child I prayed; and the Lord has granted me my petition which I made to him. Therefore I have lent him to the Lord; as long as he lives, he is lent to the Lord" (I Samuel 1:26–28).

I put Samuel's tiny hand into the gnarled fingers of Eli. I smiled with reassurance as his young eyes looked at me with uncertainty. "Remember what I have taught you, son: you belong to the Lord; your duty is to serve him. Mother and father will come to see you every year. Go now with Eli the priest and serve the Lord in whatever ways he asks."

I do not deny that there was a tug in my heart as I watched Eli lead my son, my only son, into the tents where the priests lived. I do not deny that I faced the homeward trip with reluctance, knowing that a whole year would go by before I would see that pudgy face and hear that lilting voice.

But God had honored my petition, and I had to honor my vow.

I lived that scene again as I gave the new robe a final inspection. I held it up for Elkanah to admire, before I carefully packed it for the journey to Shiloh. How I loved that journey now! With what zest would I eat the sacrificial meal—and the special portions Elkanah would give me now that God had heard my prayer. To worship God and to see Samuel were the great joys of my life. Year by year Eli has told me of Samuel's growth, of his understanding of God's law, of his special call to be God's servant, of his obedience to the commands of God. Seeing Samuel enriches my worship, as he reminds me of the goodness and greatness of Israel's Lord.

There is a special song that I sing when I go to Shiloh, a song that I first sang the year I left Samuel with Eli. It is a song of victory, like the song of Miriam and Moses on the east bank of the Red Sea. Year after year I sing it with increasing zest as I meditate on the glory of our God.

"My heart exults in the Lord;
    my strength is exalted in the Lord.
My mouth derides my enemies,
    because I rejoice in thy salvation."

(I Samuel 2:1)

A God greater than all our enemies is on our side. That is the theme of my song. The God who smashed the forces of Pharaoh, the God who confounded the defenses of Jericho, the God who drenched the troops of Sisera, the God who confused the hosts of Midian, the God who crushed the nobles of Philistia in the temple of the god Dagon had rescued me from the enemies who mocked my barrenness.

A God unique among the gods is on our side:

"There is none holy like the Lord,
    there is none besides thee;
    there is no rock like our God."

(I Samuel 2:2)

Who else can dry up a sea? Who else can smash strong walls? Who else can defeat a mighty army with a handful of torches and trumpets? Who else can speak life into a barren woman's womb?

A God famous for his surprises is on our side:

"The bows of the mighty are broken,
    but the feeble gird on strength.

The barren has borne seven,
    but she who has many children
    is forlorn."

(I Samuel 2:4,5)

The halting words of Moses live in the hearts of God's people, while Pharaoh's eloquence is forgotten. The trumpet blasts of a bunch of nomads had more power than the fortresses of an ancient city. Blind, weak, captive, Samson outfought a Philistine host. A peasant woman from Ramah, childless for years, has borne a mighty servant of God.

The food and the animals were ready. The new robe was safely wrapped. We were on the way to Shiloh to sing praise to the God of Israel. In fact, my song had already begun.

Chapter 11

Samuel:
Prophet to Kings

And the LORD came and stood forth, calling as at other times, "Samuel! Samuel!" And Samuel said, "Speak, for thy servant hears." Then the LORD said to Samuel, "Behold, I am about to do a thing in Israel, at which the two ears of every one that hears it will tingle. On that day I will fulfill against Eli all that I have spoken concerning his house, from beginning to end. And I tell him that I am about to punish his house for ever, for the iniquity which he knew because his sons were blaspheming God, and he did not restrain them. Therefore I swear to the house of Eli that the iniquity of Eli's house shall not be expiated by sacrifice or offering for ever."

(I Samuel 3:10–14.)

Even as I poured out the oil I wondered. As I watched it trickle down his ruddy, beardless cheeks, I wondered. I looked at the lad before me—inexperienced, untrained, roughly clad—and I wondered. Was this barefaced shepherd boy, still breathless from running home from the fields, to be Israel's next king? Was this slip of a lad fit to take the place of the mighty Saul? Was a sheepherder from Judah, who had never been near a battle, suited to lead the armies of Israel against the Philistines? I wondered.

I found myself attracted to his beautiful, dark eyes and his handsome, suntanned cheeks, yet I still wondered. I had pictured a different sort of king when God had spoken to me: "How long will you grieve over Saul, seeing I have rejected him from being king over Israel? Fill your horn with oil, and go; I will send you to Jesse the Bethlehemite, for I have provided for myself a king among his sons" (I Samuel 16:1).

The Lord of surprises was at work again. On none of the stalwart older sons of Jesse did he lay his hand. In fact, he had rebuked my natural inclination to anoint the oldest son as king. The horn of oil had been ready in my hand. Almost instinctively I had started to raise it to pour its symbolic oil on his head. He had all the outward marks of a leader—poise, grace, strength, maturity. I had been stopped in mid-gesture, as though God himself had grasped my hand: "Do not look on his appearance or on the height of his stature, because I have rejected him; for the Lord sees not as man sees; man looks on the outward appearance, but the Lord looks on the heart" (I Samuel 16:7).

I should have known this from my own experience. As I looked into young David's bright eyes, as I sensed that boyish combination of reserve and eagerness, I saw something of myself.

God's call had come as unexpectedly to me as it had to him. I, too, had been surprised, surprised in the midst of a sound sleep. I was in Shiloh at the time, living in the temple with Eli, the old priest. In fact, the night that it happened, I was sleeping in the sanctuary near the ark. My job was to see that the sacred lamp had enough oil to burn late into the night. Suddenly I became aware that someone was calling my name: Samuel, Samuel! I stirred from sleep and ran to the priests' quarters. Old Eli was blind by this time, and it was my duty to respond to his calls and minister to his needs. I rushed to his side, only to find that he had not summoned me. Three times this happened. The strong voice called my name. Each time Eli had not uttered a sound. Finally the old priest, whom I had served since before I could remember because my mother Hannah had lent me to God, figured out who was calling. He said, "Go, lie down; and if he calls you, you shall say, 'Speak, Lord, for thy servant hears' " (I Samuel 3:9).

Eagerly, yet fearfully, I waited for the call to be repeated. This time I was ready—ready for the Lord to speak, but not ready for what he said: "Behold, I am about to do a thing in Israel, at which the two ears of every one that hears it will tingle. On that day I will fulfill against Eli all that I have spoken concerning his house, from beginning to end. And I tell him that I am about to punish his house for ever, for the iniquity which he knew, because his sons were blaspheming God, and he did not restrain them. Therefore I swear to the house of Eli that the iniquity of Eli's house shall not be expiated by sacrifice or offering for ever" (I Samuel 3: 11-14).

The next day I did my best to avoid Eli's probing questions. But to no avail. His response to my disclosure showed a remarkable serenity: "It is the Lord; let him do what seems good to him" (I Samuel 3:18). Blind, tired, aged—the priest was about to witness the collapse of his household as the dominant priestly family of Israel, and he took the news with quiet confidence in the will of God.

Transitions like these seem to have been the context of my life. Not since Joshua marched our tribes into Canaan had any single era seen such transition. Transitions in spiritual leadership, transitions in international relations, transitions in political structure—the hand of God placed me in the center of them all. Since that wondrous night when a young lad heard a strong voice, I have been thrust into a place of leadership. My task has been the difficult one of tending the flock of God through some of the most wrenching transitions in its history.

Little did I realize that the *transition in spiritual leadership* would snatch me from my quiet duties in the house of God at Shiloh and push me into prominence among the tribes of Israel. As I grew from boy to man, I sensed the presence of the Lord with me more and more. And I not only sensed his presence, I heard his voice.

In the morning hours as we offered the early sacrifices, I heard his voice promising great days for his people. As we lit the evening lamps, I heard his voice pledging his protection to his people. When the elders of the tribes came to Shiloh for counsel, I heard his voice and delivered to them his word. When the Philistines challenged us to battle, I heard his voice and relayed his orders to our military leaders. Almost before I knew it, all Israel was calling me a prophet.

What was important was not that I was a prophet, but that God was speaking to his people once again. We had felt cut off from his word. It seemed that God had turned his back on us during the years of Eli's ministry. Now he had begun to shine his face upon us as in days of old. As Moses had stood before him and heard his word, so I was called to hear and proclaim his powerful messages. As Joshua had received guidance for each phase of settlement in Canaan, so I was chosen to lead the tribes through their next great steps in God's plan to make the promised land our permanent home.

Part of God's plan was a *transition in international relationships*. For years the Philistines had been our arch-enemies. They had settled on the southern coast of Canaan about the time our fathers were freed from Egypt. In the early years of our settlement, our greatest menace was invasion by desert peoples from south and east. But for the past half century or more, the west was our vulnerable border, subject to constant pressure from the Philistines. Better organized than we were, their five great cities—Gath, Gaza, Ekron, Ashkelon, and Ashdod—often banded together to ravage our fields and orchards. Better trained than we, the Philistine soldiers often routed our troops and defiled our women. Better equipped than we, their charioteers and horsemen had weapons of iron too sharp and too strong for our weapons of bronze.

The great transition in international affairs was not the result of our military superiority. We were no match for the Philistine armies. Not, at least, until we began to call on the Lord for help. What brought us to the point of desperation was the loss of the ark of the covenant.

The news of it cost old Eli his life. When the courier announced its fearful fate, the ancient priest collapsed and died: "Israel has fled before the Philistines, and there has also been a great slaughter among the people; your two sons also, Hophni and Phinehas, are dead, and the ark of God has been captured" (I Samuel 4:17).

An incredible story! We had sent the ark of God along with our troops to protect them in battle. Now both the battle and the ark had been lost.

But the Philistines had more on their hands than they bargained for. Proudly they carried the ark to Ashdod and stored it in the temple of Dagon, their chief god. Triumphantly they entered the temple the next morning, only to find that the idol had fallen on its face before the ark of God. Not only that, but the people of Ashdod began to suffer from a plague of tumors, inflicted by the hand of God, whose shrine they held captive. From city to city the Philistines moved the ark, always with the same results— a deadly epidemic of tumors.

Finally, after seven months of such suffering, they put the ark on a new cart drawn by two milk cows and headed it east to the land of Judah. Then it was that our people recognized their true problem: not military weakness nor political confusion, but spiritual waywardness. The Lord of surprises had taught them a terrifying lesson: though he was powerful, they were not to take his power for granted. God sent his own ark away, he withdrew his own presence from his people, to teach them this lesson.

Deliverance would come only with true˜ repentance. This was the message I had sent to the tribes: "If you are returning to the Lord with all your heart, then put away the foreign gods and the Ashtaroth from among you, and direct your heart to the Lord, and serve him only, and he will deliver you out of the hand of the Philistines" (I Samuel 7:3).

The people had learned their lesson. The harsh attacks of the past decades, the ruthless slaughter of the past year, the seven empty months without the ark were enough. The Canaanite god and goddess of fertility, called Baal and Ashtaroth, were rejected. The Lord of our fathers was to be their only God.

Our spiritual reform produced military power. The Philistines' next attack was repulsed with great decisiveness. Their troops scattered like quail before wolves. From that day till this they have not ventured to invade our land. More than that, they have restored to us all the cities along our borders which they had captured through the long years of struggle. The deliverance which God had promised so long ago to Samson's parents, Manoah and his wife, was now complete.

My work, however, was not. I thought of this as I poured out the oil on the young shepherd. This act of anointing was part of another transition in which I was called to take leadership—*the transition from judgeship to kingship*. Abortive attempts along this line had been made earlier. Gideon had refused the people's efforts to make him king, though his son Abimelech had readily volunteered. Eli's sons, no doubt, had designs on the office before their defeat by the Philistines. And so, I fear, did my own sons. But God would have no part in any of these ambitious plots, for he was Israel's King. Any true ruler of his people must be chosen by him, as Moses and Joshua were, and as I had been. And any true ruler had to walk in his ways, as Eli's sons—and my sons—had refused to do.

My heart went out to the shepherd boy. As the oil splashed on his head and ran down his neck, I prayed. I remembered so vividly another anointing and what tragedy it led to. Saul was taller than David, a giant of a man. Full of hope and promise he had stood before me, a prince of Benjamin, a stalwart man of Israel. Now he was to be replaced.

His pride of power, his rashness of judgment, his heat of temper—all these had disqualified him to be king of God's people. Saul had taken the kings of Canaan—proud, bold, cruel—as his pattern. His days were numbered.

The God of surprises was at work again. The mighty man was to be put down; the shepherd lad was to be raised up. The God who had sent Isaac to the womb of Sarah when she was too old to bear children, the God who had provided a ram when Isaac was about to be sacrificed, the God who lifted Joseph from prisoner to prime minister, the God who lit a bush as a signal for Moses, the God who paved the valley of the Jordan River and leveled the fortress of Jericho, the God of Gideon's trumpets and Jael's tent pin, the God of my barren mother was still working his surprises.

I watched as the oil trickled down David's shoulders. I watched and wondered. But I did more. I remembered and hoped.

Chapter 12

Saul:
King Who Failed

Now the day before Saul came, the LORD had revealed to Samuel: "Tomorrow about this time I will send to you a man from the land of Benjamin, and you shall anoint him to be prince over my people Israel. He shall save my people from the hand of the Philistines; for I have seen the affliction of my people because their cry has come to me." When Samuel saw Saul, the LORD told him, "Here is the man of whom I spoke to you! He it is who shall rule over my people." (I Samuel 9:15–17.)

I would have given everything I owned to begin again. The bleeding bodies that covered the slopes of Mt. Gilboa were silent, yet eloquent, reminders of my mistakes. We had scrambled our way to the summit, my sons and I, but the Philistines were not to be denied. Their archers clambered up the hillsides like the conies I used to hunt in my boyhood days in the gentle hills of Benjamin.

Now I was the hunted. No army could claim a higher prize than the head of a king. I had no doubt that before sunset my head would be a grim trophy in the Philistines' camp that I could see stretched out below in the plain of Jezreel.

I would have given everything to begin again. My army was decimated. The enemy that had plagued our western cities for years was now firmly encamped in the heart of our northern territory. By controlling Jezreel they had effectively cut off our hope of reinforcements from either north or south. My strategy had been to fight in the hills, rather than on the plain where the Philistine chariots would give their troops a greater advantage.

But my strategy had failed. We were beaten by our own tactics. My soldiers, who had always been at home in those hills, proved powerless before the Philistine forces that had been whipped to a fevered frenzy by their mounting success. The sharpest reminder of my failure was not the dark lines of Philistine soldiers that wound like thread up the sides of Gilboa; it was not their proud camp where tents dotted the fertile valley of Jezreel to the west; it was not the smoke of a dozen towns like Bethshan, Shunem, and Endor, where even now widows and orphans were wailing over their dead. The sharpest reminder of my failure was the sight of my three sons lying lifeless on the mountainside. No heir of mine would mount my throne; no son of mine would wear my armor; no child of mine would carry on my name.

My armor bearer and I stood alone. Our time was short. The Philistine archers left us no route of retreat. As I stared death in the face, I would have given everything to begin again. *Dying* was not the problem. I had had many skirmishes with death throughout the years of my soldiering. What plagued me most in those last moments was that everything I had touched had turned sour. Every hope I had held out for my kingdom had been dashed.

Old Samuel had been right. He had been right that day when I grabbed his robe and tore it. Samuel seized this as a sign: "The Lord has torn the kingdom of Israel from you this day, and has given it to a neighbor of yours, who is better than you. And also the Glory of Israel [that was what Samuel called God] will not lie or repent; for he is not a man, that he should repent" (I Samuel 15:28-29).

How I had clutched at the kingdom to prove Samuel wrong. No one could convince me that I was not the best man to rule. Among the tribes of Israel no man could march further and fight harder than I. But all of this had been to no avail. Neither my stature, head and shoulders above my countrymen, nor my reputation would save me now. God was ready to enforce the change that Samuel had predicted. My rule that had begun with so much promise was now to end with so much shame.

There had been great promise at the beginning. Samuel's actions had taken me completely by surprise, when he took a vial of oil and poured it on my head: "Has not the Lord anointed you to be prince over his people Israel? And you shall reign over the people of the Lord and you will save them from the hand of their enemies round about" (I Samuel 10:1).

Samuel's misgivings about the kingship had been well known to all of us. I had heard Kish, my father, discuss them with the other elders in the city gate. The old prophet had made clear that a king would impose his own will on the tribes and curtail their freedom: "He will take your sons and appoint them to his chariots and to be his horse-men, and to run before his chariots. . . . He will take your daughters to be perfumers and cooks and bakers. He will take the best of your fields and vineyards and olive or-chards and give them to his servants. . . . And in that day you will cry out because of your king, whom you have chosen for yourselves; but the Lord will not answer you in that day" (I Samuel 8:11, 13-14, 18).

Samuel's misgivings were what had made me reluctant, at first, to accept the office. Like Samuel, I knew that the people wanted a king for the wrong reasons. Stubbornly they refused to listen to his words; brashly they brushed aside his advice. "No! but we will have a king over us, that we also may be like all the nations, and that our king may govern us and go out before us and fight our battles" (I Samuel 8:19-20). I could sense the tension between those who agreed with the prophet and those who demanded a king. Like opposing battle lines they were arrayed, bows stretched and arrows mounted. I had no desire to put myself in the line of fire. That was why I had hidden behind the baggage at Mizpah, where the tribes had gathered for my coronation.

Half chagrined and half exhilarated I had stood before the people as the prophet found me and singled me out: "Do you see him whom the Lord has chosen? There is none like him among all the people." At Samuel's words a shout thundered forth that shook the hillsides, "Long live the king!" (I Samuel 10:24).

Ironic that I should recall those words now that I have so little time to live. That distant shout will so soon be lost in the brutal cheers of the Philistines when my severed head and mangled body are paraded through their camp.

I had tried at first to heed Samuel's stern warning and not become a despot like the kings of Canaan. I had held my peace when some rabble rousers questioned my right to rule. I had restrained my men from slaughtering those rebels after our first great victory over Nahash, the Ammonite. I had even made sure that the Lord got credit for that military triumph. "Not a man shall be put to death this day," I had commanded, "for today the Lord has wrought deliverance in Israel" (I Samuel 11:13).

The transition to my rulership had been no easier for Samuel than it had for me. The people's cry for a king he had interpreted as their rejection of his leadership as well as of the Lord's. He had been eager both to vindicate his own ministry and to safeguard mine. In a form of farewell assembly he had summoned the tribes to Gilgal and had addressed them on his ministry and mine: "Behold, I have hearkened to your voice in all that you have said to me, and have made a king over you. . . . Here I am; testify against me before the Lord and before his anointed (God's 'anointed' was the way Samuel often referred to me). Whose ox have I taken? Or whose ass have I taken? Or whom have I defrauded? Whom have I oppressed? Or from whose hand have I taken a bribe to blind my eyes with it? Testify against me and I will restore it to you." The people's response must have gratified the old man:

"You have not defrauded us or oppressed us or taken anything from any man's hand" (I Samuel 12:1, 3-4).

Indeed, he had not. Would that I could have said the same, as I watched the Philistine archers climb Gilboa with murder in their eyes! And would that I had heeded the prophet's sound counsel: "If you will fear the Lord and serve him and hearken to his voice and not rebel against the commandment of the Lord, and if both you and the king who reigns over you will follow the Lord your God, it will be well" (I Samuel 12:14).

Try as I had at first to walk in God's ways, my rashness and my arrogance got the best of me on two key occasions. The first time it had happened was at Gilgal. For seven days my troops and I had waited for Samuel. We had no intent to march against the Philistines until he had come to offer sacrifices for us. We knew that without God's blessing our campaign would miscarry. Finally, I had taken matters into my own hands and offered the burnt offering to God. As the smoke curled heavenward, Samuel had arrived, full of righteous wrath. I, the anointed king, had also seized the office of the priest when I put the torch to the sacrifice. Samuel's response had been uncompromising: "You have done foolishly; you have not kept the commandment of the Lord your God, which he commanded you; for now the Lord would have established your kingdom over Israel for ever. But now your kingdom shall not continue; the Lord has sought out a man after his own heart; and the Lord has appointed him to be prince over his people, because you have not kept what the Lord commanded you" (I Samuel 13:13-14).

Even the king has a King! That had been the lesson Samuel wished me to learn. Learn it I did on the second occasion when my rashness got the upper hand. I had marshaled the largest Israelite army in recent history to crush the Amalekites, who troubled our southern borders perpetually like a nagging thorn in a lion's paw. Samuel had ordered us to destroy everyone and everything we captured, as a mammoth sacrifice to God. But again I had taken the law into my own hands and spared Agag, the king, and the best animals of his flocks.

Samuel was furious, especially when I lied and told him the destruction had been total. Not even my excuse that I had spared the animals to make personal sacrifices to God could cool his anger. I can still hear his words:

"Has the Lord as great delight in
    burnt offerings and sacrifices,
        as in obeying the voice of the Lord?
Behold, to obey is better than sacrifice,
    and to hearken than the fat of rams.
For rebellion is as the sin of divination,
    and stubbornness is as iniquity and idolatry.
Because you have rejected the word of the Lord,
    he has also rejected you from being king."

                                    (I Samuel 15:22–23)

It was shortly after that rebuke that my whole personality changed. Fits of depression and temper seized me frequently. I felt disturbed, distraught, unsettled.

The peace, the poise, the power that God's Spirit had brought to me when Samuel first anointed me were gone. In their stead, anger, despair, and jealousy reigned. The only thing that would quiet my distress was music.

That was how I first met David. On the advice of one of my young men, I had summoned him to court. Whenever my spirit seemed to be haunted by that evil spirit, I called for him to play and sing.

But even there, my jealousy had run away with me. Perhaps it was David's victory over the gigantic Philistine warrior—Goliath, I think his name was. Perhaps it was David's friendship with my son Jonathan, who spent more and more time with him. More likely my jealousy was sparked by reports that David, not one of my sons, was to be the next king. Rumor had it that Samuel had already anointed him to take my place. He became a popular hero, which made things worse. How I reddened with rage when the women celebrated his victory over Goliath with these words:

"Saul has slain his thousands,
    and David his ten thousands." (I Samuel 18:7)

For whatever reason, perhaps for all these reasons, my jealousy of David made life wretched for me and for him. Killing him became the obsession of my life. All my plans were made, all my decisions were taken, all my moves were plotted with one aim in mind—to kill him.

But now I was to die first. And he was to rule. Samuel had been right. The kingship was full of risks—oppression,

ambition, abuse of power, compromise of Israel's uniqueness. In each of these I had failed.

The Philistines drew near. Their arrows began to land
near our feet. I would prefer to die by my own hand
rather than by theirs. One last look from Mt. Gilboa reminds me of the scope and beauty of our land. I would
give everything to start over.

God wills otherwise. I have had my day. But his day
goes on. His kingdom will be established. God has already
laid his hand on the new king. I pray that he will be a
king who lets the God of Israel be the King of kings.

Chapter 13

David:
King After God's Heart

"When your days are fulfilled and you lie down with your fathers, I will raise up your son after you, who shall come forth from your body, and I will establish his kingdom. He shall build a house for my name, and I will establish the throne of his kingdom forever. I will be his father, and he shall be my son. When he commits iniquity, I will chasten him with the rod of men, with the stripes of the sons of men; but I will not take my steadfast love from him, as I took it from Saul, whom I put away from before you. And your house and your kingdom shall be made sure forever before me; your throne shall be established forever." (II Samuel 7:12–16.)

With the rebellion put down I could now give myself to the last important assignment of my life. For almost forty years I have been working to bind these twelve tribes of ours into a strong and stable nation. And twice within the past year or so my people have been scarred by the wounds of rebellion.

Now Sheba, that worthless son of Benjamin's tribe, has been dealt with. He it was who blew the trumpet of revolt that bode to strip me of the support of the northern tribes. Because I was a southerner, a native of Bethlehem in Judah's territory, the northern tribes at times felt less kinship with me than I wished. And Sheba tried to stampede them into a massive act of disloyalty:

"We have no portion in David,
    and we have no inheritance in the son of Jesse;
    everyman to his tents, O Israel!" (II Samuel 20:1)

He succeeded. The men of Israel did abandon me and return to their homes.

Sheba's success was partly my fault. I had slighted the men of the north when I returned in triumph to Jerusalem after days of exile across the Jordan. I had asked the men of Judah to escort me into the city, despite the fact that many of them sided with my son Absalom in his ill-fated rebellion. Miffed at my decision, the troops of the ten northern tribes quarrelled with the men of Judah. That rift cleared the way for Sheba's foolish insurrection.

It was Joab who put down the rebellion with the aid of the citizens of Abel, a town in the far north about a day's journey from Damascus. Sheba had fled there to rally support for his revolt. But Joab tracked him as a wolf would hunt a rabbit and persuaded the men and women of Abel to seize him, lest their town be devoured by Joab's men.

With Sheba dead, I am free to get on with the task of preparing the kingdom for the transition that will take place as I go to sleep with my fathers. Nothing can be more important to a king than the assurance that his people—as close to him as his own flesh and blood—will be well cared for by his successor.

Successor—that very word stabs at me more sharply than any Philistine sword. I thought I knew who would succeed me as head of the twelve tribes. From the beginning, my son Absalom seemed to wear all the graces that make for leadership. Charm, intelligence, energy, beauty—all of these he had in abundance. In all Israel there was no one so much to be praised for his beauty as Absalom; from the sole of his foot to the crown of his head there was no blemish in him. And his hair grew with a luxury akin to that of the vineyards of Eshcol, where Moses' spies first sensed the fruitfulness of the promised land.

I suppose it was his charm that proved Absalom's undoing. Sensing his winning ways, he set out to steal the hearts of the people. A champion of justice he pretended to be, promising a fair trial to all who came to court with grievances. By the hundreds the people rallied to him, stirred by his pledges and wooed by his winsomeness.

Then it happened. Carefully calculating his support, he withdrew to Hebron and proclaimed himself as king. What would have come to him in due course he had no patience to wait for. Impetuously he tried to clutch the crown from his own father's graying head. And to my surprise and chagrin he came within a hair's breadth of succeeding.

Backed by troops from Judah and other tribes, Absalom so threatened the peace of my capital that I had to flee to the wilderness east of Jordan. As the messengers risked their necks to smuggle daily reports across the river, hope of any peaceful settlement grew dim. Finally when Absalom marched his forces to Jordan, the battle had to be joined. Reluctantly I sent my armies forth to meet my son, with only this word of command to my three generals: "Deal gently for my sake with the young man Absalom" (II Samuel 18:5).

Wasted words these were, for the sternness of my general Joab rode roughshod over the sentiment of a father. At the close of the fierce battle, when twenty thousand troops had perished, Absalom tried to escape on his mule. A low-hanging branch from a thick oak tree snared his massive head of hair and dangled him by his tresses like a sheepskin drying in the wind, while his dazed mule stumbled on.

The news of victory was drowned in the grief over Absalom's death at the hands of Joab. When the full impact of it hit me I could do nothing more than wail the

strong lament: "O my son Absalom, my son, my son
Absalom! Would I had died instead of you, O Absalom,
my son, my son!" (II Samuel 18:33). Not since my boyhood friend Jonathan had perished at the side of his father,
King Saul, had my eyes known such tears and my spirit
such emptiness. Just recounting it revives an ache almost
beyond bearing.

Now both rebellions have been put down—Absalom's
and Sheba's—and both rebels have gone the way of all
flesh. A peaceful passing of the crown, a gentle transfer
of the throne is what I seek.

How heavily the responsibility has rested on my shoulders. Chafing like an oaken yoke on an ox's neck, it has
determined the course of my life since that day when
Jesse, my father, fetched me from following his flock and
stood me before Samuel, the prophet. Anointed to be king,
I carried that burden through the fitful, fretful years that
ended Saul's reign. Sometimes as Saul's ally and sometimes as his enemy, I waited for our God to fulfill the old
prophet's promise. I waited, and I wondered.

Spared by God from Saul's wrath and supported by my
seasoned band of comrades, I waited for my time to come.
And when it came, I dreaded it. For the news of Saul's
death—Saul the tall and handsome one, Saul the great
uniter of the scattered tribes, Saul the menace to the Philistine intruders—the news of his death brought me no joy.

Yet someone had to reign; someone had to keep the
scattered tribes from fragmenting; someone had to show
an iron hand and an iron will to match the iron weapons
of the Philistines. It was the command of the Lord that
sent me up to Hebron to be anointed again—this time by
the men of Judah. In that old town that cast its shadow
on the tombs of Abraham and the other fathers and
mothers of our tribes, in that old town that Caleb had
wrested from the Anakim in Joshua's day, I ascended first
to the command of Judah and later to the leadership of
the northern tribes as well.

Saul's family did not easily give up their claims to the
crown. But God blessed me and my men while Ishbaal,
Saul's son, and Abner, who prodded him on in his grasping ways, were turned aside. The throne of the twelve
sons of Jacob belonged to me.

But it became no resting place. War became my way of
life. Since that memorable hour when the stone from my

shepherd's sling felled Goliath, the Philistine hero, fighting had been my occupation. Goliath was but the first of a host of mighty warriors to fall before my weapons as Lebanon's giant cedars crash before the axes of Hiram's timbermen.

With Saul's death, the Philistines lusted for fresh conquests. Their plan was to take advantage of the confusion caused by the changing of leadership and to press north and east into the towns of Judah and Benjamin. They knew me well from the days when I had lived among them and had sometimes served their causes.

But I knew them well, too. I knew their pagan religion, their selfish ambition, and their cruel practices. I knew the terrain where the battles would be waged; I had lived off that land in the days when Saul had me on the run. I knew the tactics of the Philistine commanders; I had fought side by side with them in many a skirmish. More important, I knew that God was with me. Twice Philistine invasions were repelled by the skill of my armies and the might of the Lord of hosts.

With some semblance of security in the land, my next task was to establish a capital that would pull the tribes together. Shechem was too far north, detached from Judah, and Hebron was too far south, isolated from Ephraim and the other northern tribes. But between them lay just the place, a great cluster of hills and valleys, called Jerusalem. The Jebusites held it then and had since before Joshua conquered the promised land. The Jebusites were a tribe of Canaanites, whose hilly fortress had resisted all prior attempts at conquest. The lame and the blind of Jerusalem will be sufficient troops to hold you off, was the taunt they hurled at me.

But the Lord marched with me, and my men breached the defenses of the city by climbing up the water shaft. Jerusalem was mine, a capital fit for Israel's tribes, a city beautiful for situation.

And the defeat of the Jebusites was just the beginning. From that mountain citadel we marched—my tested soldiers and I—into Moab and Syria, into Edom and Ammon. Every border of ours I extended—east, south, and north. Taking full advantage of the weak regimes in both Egypt and Mesopotamia, I controlled Palestine and its neighboring states in the name of the Lord.

Though war had been my chief occupation, it was not

my chief delight. Worship was. My heart was fixed on the God of the covenant, the God who had pledged himself to our tribes, the God who had hurried us from Egypt and settled us in Canaan, the God who had comforted and strengthened me in my shepherd days in Bethlehem, the God who had called me to serve his people, the God who had judged me and forgiven me of my dark sins against Bathsheba and Uriah her husband, the God who had broken the rebel spears of Absalom and Sheba.

The worship of the true and living God in whose name I had gloried in so many songs—that worship became my high aim. I was a king whose name was noised abroad from Babylon to Thebes, from Hamath to Petra. Yet I was a king under orders, a king who was a servant.

The Egyptian kings believed themselves to be incarnations of their sun god, but I knew just how mortal and human my flesh was. The memory of my adultery and murder would not let me forget. The kings of Canaan who ruled these great cities before me thought that they had sucked the breasts of their goddess to drink the milk of divinity, but I knew well my foolishness and frailty. My rash act of taking a census in order to test the financial and military strength of my people taught me just how dependent on the Lord I was.

Not an incarnate god like the Pharaohs, not a divine man like the Canaanites, I was a servant of God and my people—a servant under orders to worship and to obey. That was why I wanted to bring to Jerusalem the ark of God, which is called by the name of the Lord of hosts who sits enthroned on the cherubim.

What a procession that was! The ark rocked majestically as its new cart lumbered forward as though in step to the beat of our songs. Spirited strumming of the harps and lyres, fervent shaking of the tambourines and castanets and vigorous banging of the cymbals—those were the accompaniments to the march and to the dance. And, oh, how we danced before the Lord! My tired bones leap for joy at the memory.

Awed by his power, we danced; overjoyed by his presence, we danced; flooded with gratitude for his provision, we danced. And then we sacrificed. Burnt offerings of young bulls we sacrificed; peace offerings of lambs we sacrificed. And all the people joined me in blessing the name of the Lord of hosts.

From that day to this the ark has rested in Jerusalem. And to it have come on the great festal occasions—passover, day of the first fruits, and tabernacles—the men and women of the tribes to join me in worship. From Dan they have journeyed south and from Beersheba they have walked north to glorify the name of the Lord whose glory dwells among us.

One day the ark will have a great house to shelter it. But that will be up to my son. Settling Solomon on the throne must be the last great act of my reign. Could I grant him one grand wish, it would not be success in battle. I have had more than enough of that. It would not be prestige before the neighbor kings; they have all spread their tribute at my feet. My one great wish would be a faithful heart to worship the Lord God of our fathers. Without that, all kings and kingdoms will ultimately crumble like a brittle pot shattered by the iron rod of judgment.

Chapter 14

Bathsheba:
Queen Mother of Judah

So Bathsheba went to the king into his chamber (now the king was very old, and Abishag the Shunammite was ministering to the king). Bathsheba bowed and did obeisance to the king, and the king said, "What do you desire?" She said to him, "My lord, you swore to your maidservant by the Lord your God, saying, 'Solomon your son shall reign after me, and he shall sit upon my throne.' And now, behold Adonijah is king, although you, my lord the king, do not know it. He has sacrificed oxen, fatlings, and sheep in abundance, and has invited all the sons of the king, Abiathar the priest, and Joab the commander of the army; but Solomon your servant he has not invited. And now, my lord the king, the eyes of all Israel are upon you, to tell them who shall sit on the throne of my lord the king after him." (I Kings 1:15–20.)

His very name meant "peace". That was why I had begged David to make Solomon king in his stead. Any other choice would have led to unspeakable suffering. The streets of Jerusalem would have run with blood.

Adonijah, Solomon's rival, was just that kind of man. Power was his goal, and he would have paid any price to get it. Older than Solomon, born to David's wife Haggith before David conquered Jerusalem, Adonijah thought the throne would be his automatically.

Perhaps automatically is too strong a word, for Adonijah had to take things into his own hands. David was in his last days, too old to move about much and subject to continual cold. The winter of his life left him unable to stay warm, no matter what garments his servants clothed him with. So we brought Abishag, a young maiden from the village of Shunem in the north, to be David's constant companion. We hoped that the warmth of her young body and the tenderness of her daily care would bring rest and comfort to the aged king.

Adonijah took this move as a sign that David was about to go to his fathers. With high ambition, he mustered a band of men and a handful of chariots and set out to form a court.

He had good help. Joab, David's crafty general sided with Adonijah, and so did Abiathar, the priest. What at first seemed wild rumors soon became verified reports. Adonijah went so far as to invite the leaders of Jerusalem to the old Serpent Stone at En-rogel, just a few minutes' walk from the city, where he offered sacrifices in what was virtually a coronation ceremony.

Then it was that Nathan, the wise old prophet, and I had to take strong steps to block Adonijah's moves. At stake were our own lives. Though handsome and personable, Adonijah could also be cruel and ruthless. As his father grew weaker, Adonijah's ambitions swelled like a wadi in flood and threatened to wash Solomon, Nathan, and me away in its swirling waters.

But it was more than fear for our own safety that moved Nathan and me to intervene. We feared revolt on the part of the citizens of Jerusalem. Solomon was a son of their city, born and raised on its proud hills. The people of

Jerusalem—Jebusites and Israelites alike—felt a greater
kinship to Solomon than to Adonijah, who was already a
strapping lad when David moved his capital from Hebron
to Jerusalem.

One other factor shaped our plan. Solomon's name
meant "peace," "welfare." And his personality suited his
name. A poet like his father, he took little interest in
military pursuits. A lengthy reign of his might well mark
an age of peace, a period of strong government to stabil-
ize the restless tribes, a time of trading and treaty. What
David had conquered Solomon could consolidate. And
Israel—God's special people—might have their finest era.

Nathan, to whom the Lord spoke so clearly and so
often, seemed to agree. As David's closest counselor, as
the greatest prophet since Samuel, his word counted with
the king. Confronted by the pleas of both of us, David
moved rapidly to install Solomon on the throne.

I admired the courage of the old man. He had met so
many challenges—from Ishbaal and Abner at the beginning, from Absalom and Sheba at the height of his power
—yet he was ready for one more. These were his words:
"As the Lord lives, who has redeemed my soul out of
every adversity, as I swore to you by the Lord, the God
of Israel, saying, 'Solomon your son shall reign after me,
and he shall sit upon my throne in my stead'; even so will
I do this day" (I Kings 1:29-30).

As I rose from bowing before the king, I could see
Nathan nodding his head in approval. I knew what he was
thinking. His memory drifted back to a day when the Lord
had given him a special message for David and David's
people. The stern old prophet seemed to be rehearsing the
words he had voiced to David so many years before:
"When your days are fulfilled and you lie down with your
fathers, I will raise up your offspring after you, who shall
come forth from your body, and I will establish his kingdom. He shall build a house for my name, and I will
establish the throne of his kingdom for ever. I will be his
father, and he shall be my son" (II Samuel 7:12-14).
Nathan's nod told the whole story. Solomon, he had no
doubt, was the fulfillment of that prophecy.

At Gihon, the sacred spring east of Jerusalem, the
coronation took place. And with great pageantry. Solomon rode to the scene on his father's mule. Zadok the
priest and Nathan the prophet were on hand to do the

anointing. David's crack troops, the private company of Philistine bodyguards who had served him all their lives, were on hand as escorts. The shout that rose from the people—"Long live King Solomon"—sounded like an alarm in the camp of Adonijah and signaled the end of his play for the throne.

At least that was what I thought. In fact, so thoroughly did I think that Adonijah had been outwitted by Nathan and me that I almost felt sorry for him. That was what made me blind to his final grasp at the throne. When David slept with his fathers and was buried, Adonijah came to speak with me about Abishag, David's comely companion during his final days. Adonijah's plea seemed straightforward: "You know that the kingdom was mine, and that all Israel fully expected me to reign; however the kingdom has turned about and become my brother's, for it was his from the Lord. And now I have one request to make of you; do not refuse me. . . . Pray ask King Solomon —he will not refuse you—to give me Abishag the Shunammite as my wife." Thinking the request to be harmless, I replied, "Very well; I will speak for you to the king" (I Kings 2:15-18).

Solomon was furious; he snapped at me like a fierce dog: "And why do you ask Abishag the Shunammite for Adonijah? Ask for him the kingdom also" (I Kings 2:22). Then it dawned on me. Adonijah wanted to use Abishag as a stepping-stone to the throne. On his side he already had his seniority over Solomon and the backing of Abiathar and Joab, two leaders highly respected in Israel. All he would need to dislodge Solomon would be Abishag as his wife. To the men and women of Israel she would symbolize his right to succeed David. After all, she had been the old king's closest companion to the day of his death.

Solomon sensed this and took quick action. The news of Adonijah's execution left me shocked and gratified— shocked at the death of another son of David, gratified that Solomon's position was secured. He could now get on with his pursuit of the peace that his name had promised.

What peace that name had first brought to me! Solomon's birth itself was a word of grace from the living God. Our first baby—David's and mine—had lived only a few days. The hand of God had been heavy on him and on us.

And for good reasons. The whole story is painful to

recount. It began with my indiscretion in bathing myself in view of the king's house. My beauty was more than he could resist; and his authority was more than I could refuse.

So it happened. Adultery—there was no other name for it. All my hopes of keeping the act private were dashed when a few weeks later I knew I was pregnant. It was David's child beyond doubt. Uriah, my husband, was with David's troops in Ammon, east of Jordan, and had not been with me for weeks. Though a descendant of a Hittite family that had been in Jerusalem for generations, Uriah was loyal to Jerusalem's new king and was a responsible officer among David's men.

David scarcely spoke to me when I told him of the unborn child. Instead he dispatched to Joab, his commander in Moab, a message whose contents he did not reveal to me. The next thing I heard was a report that my husband had been summoned from the battlefield and ordered to report to the king.

But I did not see him. Only after several days did the full story reach me. And then it was too late: Uriah was dead.

My tears of grief dissolved the glue that sealed David's lips, and with great pain he told me what had happened. He had tried to get Uriah to visit me while he was on leave from battle. But he would not. Why, we did not know. The reason Uriah gave was that it would be sacrilege for him to enjoy the love of his wife while the ark and the troops of Israel were in the field waging war in the Lord's name. Was that the real reason? I have always wondered. Had Uriah gotten wind of David's deed and the child that he conceived? Was anger with me or vengeance on David his reason for refusing the opportunity of love?

All of that was speculation now. Uriah was dead, sent back to the front lines and exposed to enemy attack at David's command.

To the shame of adultery, the king had added the guilt of murder. And he was miserable to live with. At first he tried to conceal his crime. Then Nathan the prophet confronted him with it, and the king collapsed under the weight of a smitten conscience. The champion of justice had broken the law; the guardian of the covenant had shattered one of its basic pillars; the defender of the oppressed had become the oppressor.

Humbled by the prophet's word, David waited for God's judgment to strike. He knew that no sacrifice could atone for so highhanded a sin. He threw himself on the mercy of God—a mercy that would surely show itself in judgment as Nathan had predicted.

The judgment began with its most telling blow—the death of our baby son. So distraught was David at the time that we tried to shield him from the news. When he found out, to everyone's surprise he refused to mourn and went about his business as usual. The judgment he had awaited had fallen, and he was almost relieved to have it over.

For me, the anguish lingered. David's other wives showed no mercy for my plight. Robbed of the husband whom I had loved, deprived of the child whom I had sheltered, I wondered what the future held.

Would God curse me with barrenness for my part in David's sin? Would the king discard me in order to escape the memory of his shame? Would Israel, shaken to its roots by the crimes of its king, ever be at peace again?

It was while my heart was struggling with questions like those that my body stirred again with new life. And a few short months later, Solomon was born. How I loved to say his name. It sang with hope and promise. It rang like the bells on the high priest's garment with notes of love and grace. Solomon: you could hear the word *"shalom"*—"peace"—in its very syllables. Solomon—it carried the pledge of welfare after the storms of judgment.

How we needed that pledge. David and I spoke of it when we were rocked by the news that Amnon, David's son, had raped his sister Tamar. We took comfort in the promise of Solomon's name when Absalom stole his father's concubines and tried to use their bodies to help him mount the throne. We clung to the meaning of Solomon's name in the bitter days of Sheba's rebellion as my husband, grieving over Absalom and weary of battle, had again to take to the field to secure his throne.

Now all of that was behind us, and the promise of peace was about to become a reality. There will be those who read my motive as the political ambitions of a doting mother. I have known how to use my position in court for powerful purposes. I admit that. And there may be times when I shall use my power as queen mother to influence the course of national life.

But that was not the reason why I pled Solomon's cause before his father. The reason was much simpler. Solomon had been God's sign of grace and peace to David and me in our darkest hour. His birth was a word of acceptance and forgiveness, despite all that David had done wrong. I knew in the depths of my heart that God, through Solomon, would speak that same peaceful word to all our people.

Chapter 15

Nathan:
Prophet of Wisdom
and Courage

Nathan said to David, "You are the man. Thus says the LORD, the God of Israel, 'I anointed you king over Israel, and I delivered you out of the hand of Saul; and I gave you your master's house, and your master's wives into your bosom, and gave you the house of Israel and of Judah; and if this were too little, I would add to you as much more. Why have you despised the word of the LORD, to do what is evil in his sight? You have smitten Uriah the Hittite with the sword, and have taken his wife to be your wife, and have slain him with the sword of the Ammonites. Now therefore the sword shall never depart from your house, because you have despised me, and have taken the wife of Uriah the Hittite to be your wife.'"

(II Samuel 12:7–10.)

The oil of anointing was for me the oil of gladness. As I watched the sacramental horn pour out its holy oil, the flood of joy in my heart matched the river of oil flowing down Solomon's face. This was the hour for which I had waited for nearly thirty years, the hour when I could witness the anointing of David's son as his successor.

It was a splendid scene. The spring of Gihon bubbled as we stood beside its sparkling waters. Zadok was there clad in his full priestly splendor, anointing horn in hand. Beside him were the palace guards of David, seasoned men and strong. Cherethites and Pelethites they were, tough warriors from the land of the Philistines, hardened by a hundred battles at David's side. Their ancestors had sailed from the islands of the Great Sea centuries before and had settled on the coastal plains to the west of the hills of Judah. Their presence was a token of David's good pleasure in the choice of Solomon to wear his crown.

And what a sight the young king was. Erect as a spear, alive as a stag, handsome as a lion, he looked every inch a king astride his father's royal mule. David's strength and Bathsheba's beauty—what a union they found in him!

It was a lordly scene, so different from the one David had often described to me—the one nearly fifty years ago when Samuel anointed David before an audience comprised of Jesse and David's seven brothers. It was a different scene from those at Hebron forty years before, scenes recited countless times by the old men of Judah. At Hebron a guerrilla warrior harried by the troops of Saul had responded humbly to the overtures of the people. At Gihon a bright prince reared in the palace and born to command received the cheers of the citizenry: "Long live King Solomon." The playing of the pipes, the dancing of the feet, and the joy of the shouts—regal accompaniment these were for the beginning of a golden age.

The scene was different from the others. Yet it was the same. A son from his father's loins was chosen as the people's leader. The choice was made by them, yet by more than them. Behind the coronation lay the hand of Israel's God, committed to the care of his people through the hand of a king. Behind the pouring out of the oil was the gift of God's spirit granting power to the chosen ruler.

The trappings of royalty were present at Solomon's coronation in a way that David's lacked. But the electing hand of God and the power of his Spirit—those were the true marks of royalty for Israel's kings. Adonijah, Solomon's half-brother, was encamped a scant mile away with royal trappings and with strong yearnings for the throne. But the anointing hand of God was missing. And without that no true king could be crowned.

I knew firsthand how much God cared about David and his throne. I learned that lesson forcefully one unforgettable night some years ago. The episode began when David asked my blessing on his plans to build a permanent temple to house the ark of God. I had been part of that bright processional when David had danced before the Lord as the ark jostled its way up the steep road to Jerusalem. I had heard the lyres and the harps, the cymbals and the castanets. My heart had leaped for joy when the ancient gates lifted up their heads to let the Lord of hosts, the King of glory enter.

David's zeal for a permanent, elaborate shrine I could share. I knew the importance of Israel's ark as the footstool of the Lord. No temple—even one larger and richer than the great Phoenician sanctuaries—would be too grand for the Lord God of our fathers.

Happily, eagerly, I gave my blessing to David's plan and then retired to rest. But rest I did not—not that night. As suddenly as a raven swoops on its prey, as swiftly as an eagle plummets from its crag, the word of the Lord came to me. There was no mistaking its power and clarity. What I had agreed to during the day was contradicted by God himself during the night. Not God's house but David's was the theme of that message.

Its words still ring in my ears though three momentous decades have passed since, as God's messenger, I first delivered them to David: "Thus says the Lord of hosts, I took you from the pasture, from following the sheep, that you should be prince over my people Israel; and I have been with you wherever you went, and have cut off all your enemies from before you; and I will make for you a great name, like the name of the great ones of the earth. . . . Moreover the Lord declares to you that the Lord will make you a house. When your days are fulfilled and you lie down with your fathers, I will raise up your offspring after you, who shall come forth from your body, and I will establish his kingdom. He shall build a house for my name. . . . And your house and your kingdom shall be made sure for ever before me; your throne shall be established for ever" (II Samuel 7:8-9, 11-13, 16).

David had sat in stunned silence for a time measuring with his mind the length and breadth of those words. Full well he knew what a monumental change they meant for Israel's way of life. The old pattern of the judges was replaced by a new pattern of kings. The great judges of Israel —Ehud, Shamgar, Deborah, Gideon, Samson—were chosen to rule on the basis of their gifts of leadership, not their family or lineage. They were plucked from their homes and fields by the hand of God and commissioned to rally the tribes in times of sharp emergency.

Even Saul had been chosen that way. That mountain of a man was snatched from the hills of Benjamin, where he had tended the asses of Kish his father, and was marked by God to unite the people against the peril of the Philistines. No son in the days of the judges had succeeded his father. Not even Saul's son was chosen to mount the throne —though one of them, Ishbaal, had delusions of such grandeur for a time.

Now a dynasty was to be founded, a dynasty of the sons of David. A permanent ruling family was selected by God to lead Israel into its new age—an age of unity, of power, of expansion. David was overwhelmed, visibly shaken, as I left him pondering the import of God's words.

He told me later that his only response had been to go to the tent where the ark of God was kept and to pray. What else could he have done? God had not asked for David's opinion; God had declared his own decision. There could be no argument, no discussion, only acceptance.

With gratitude David received the divine promise. Like a new part of a covenant, God had stated his will for Israel's rulership. As he had previously promised Abraham a nation, a land, and a name, he now promised David a household, a throne, a dynasty. As he had pledged to Moses that Israel would be his protected people, he now pledged to David that his family would be preserved for the sake of that people.

The king's prayer was marked by humility: "Who am I, O Lord God, and what is my house, that thou hast brought me thus far? And yet this was a small thing in thy eyes, O Lord God; thou hast spoken also of thy servant's house

for a great while to come, and hast shown me future generations, O Lord God!" (II Samuel 7:18-19).

And the king's prayer was filled with thanksgiving:
"Therefore thou art great, O Lord God; for there is none
like thee, and there is no God besides thee, according to all
that we have heard with our ears. What other nation on
earth is like thy people Israel, whom God went to redeem
to be his people, making himself a name, and doing for
them great and terrible things, by driving out before his
people a nation and its gods?" (II Samuel 7:22-23).

The king's prayer was also rich with confidence: "And
now, O Lord God, thou art God, and thy words are true,
and thou hast promised this good thing to thy servant; now
therefore may it please thee to bless the house of thy servant, that it may continue for ever before thee; for thou,
O Lord God, hast spoken, and with thy blessing shall the
house of thy servant be blessed for ever" (II Samuel
7:28-29).

As I watched the oil from Zadok's horn trickle down the
shoulders of Solomon, I remembered David's prayer with
that same humility, thanksgiving, and confidence. The first
stage in the fulfilling of those promises was at hand, and my
heart sang of the faithfulness of God.

There had been times when I had wondered whether that
household which I prophesied would truly come to pass.
No, it was not the military challenge of Israel's neighbors
that threatened the dynasty. One by one, David's military
prowess and God's mighty presence did them in. Philistines,
Edomites, Moabites, Ammonites, Amalekites, and Syrians
—all of them learned to fear the march of Israel's feet and
the wrath of Israel's God. Even the hosts of Egypt to the
south and Mesopotamia to the east were not strong enough
to make David their servant. Lord of all he surveyed he
found himself.

Nor was it internal rebellion that posed the greatest
danger to David's proud monarchy. Absalom and Sheba,
vicious though they were, were ultimately no match for the
old warrior, who had tested his skills and learned his tactics
before either of them was born.

Lord of all he surveyed was David—except of himself.
His darkest hour came not in the smoke of battle, but on a
clear, warm spring afternoon when he stayed home.

Then it was that Bathsheba's charms conquered him. A
look from his rooftop and then another, longer look were

more than he could bear. He had the power to take her but not the discipline to keep that power in rein. Like a charging steed in Pharaoh's chariotry, his passions rode away with him. And his adultery soon led to murder, as David saw to it that Uriah, Bathsheba's husband, was struck down in battle.

Once again the Lord disturbed me with a message for the king. This time there was no excitement as I went to bear it—only anxiety. With my heart sick within me, I stood before my friend and sovereign.

A story was the way God had chosen to get his point across—a story about sheep to catch the ear of an old shepherd, and a story about justice to trap the conscience of an old judge. I began to tell it as firmly and as calmly as I could: "There were two men in a certain city, the one rich and the other poor. The rich man had very many flocks and herds; but the poor man had nothing but one little ewe lamb, which he had bought. And he brought it up, and it grew up with him and with his children; it used to eat of his morsel, and drink from his cup, and lie in his bosom, and it was like a daughter to him. Now there came a traveler to the rich man, and he was unwilling to take one of his own flock or herd to prepare for the wayfarer who had come to him, but he took the poor man's lamb, and prepared it for the man who had come to him" (II Samuel 12:1-4).

I had scarcely finished the story, when I had the result I wanted. David was furious: "As the Lord lives, the man who has done this deserves to die; and he shall restore the lamb fourfold, because he did this thing, and because he had no pity" (II Samuel 12:5-6).

That was my moment. The king had given me my opening, and I thrust my words at him like a sword: "You are the man" (II Samuel 7:7). David collapsed under the burden of his guilt, like the temple at Gaza shaken by the strength of Samson. I heaved a huge sigh of relief. My mission was accomplished. The king had repented. He too was subject to God's laws, and he had acknowledged that subjection. Judgment there would have to be, but the household promised by God would be secure.

I relived those chilling moments as I heard the men and women at Gihon's spring raise their shout: "Long live Solomon the king." David's loyalty to God, which was his greatest attribute, had been vindicated. The man of grand

failure yet of great faith had seen his last wish come true.
What Bathsheba and I had urged him to do, he had done.
Solomon had been chosen king and now anointed. The succession to the throne had been assured.

I suppose deep down I had known it would be, despite
the fleeting doubts in those dark hours of David's sin. The
mighty word of God that had stirred me from my rest and
impelled me to deliver God's promises to David was at
work all the time. That word overcame obstacles, destroyed
doubt, and shaped destinies. It was the same word that had
created the heavens and the earth. The word of the Lord.
It had to come true. God himself saw to it. And the anointing oil poured out on Solomon's head was the sign that God
had said yes to his promise. But then does he not always
do that?

Chapter 16

———

Solomon:
King of the Golden Age

Now Hiram king of Tyre sent his servants to Solomon, when he heard that they had anointed him king in place of his father; for Hiram always loved David. And Solomon sent word to Hiram, "You know that David my father could not build a house for the name of the Lord his GOD because of the warfare with which his enemies surrounded him, until the LORD put them under the soles of his feet. But now the Lord my GOD has given me rest on every side; there is neither adversary nor misfortune. And so I purpose to build a house for the name of the Lord my GOD, as the LORD said to David my father, 'Your son, whom I will set upon your throne in your place, shall build the house for my name.'" (I Kings 5:1–5.)

If I had it to do over again, there are many things I would do differently. My life has been a long cord woven of satisfaction and regret. There are strands that I would like to weave again, but such opportunities do not come to us as mortal men. We do our weaving, leave our cords behind us, and pass on to sleep with our fathers.

Forty years have come and gone since that day when Zadok the priest and Nathan the prophet proclaimed me king beside the spring of Gihon. Our country is a very different place from what I found it when my father David died. Even a casual stroll through Jerusalem would show what I mean.

Take the marketplace, for instance. What a bustle of activity it is, as the wealthy women bargain for the exotic goods on display. Spices, perfumes, ointments, and cloth from the corners of the world are available since I opened up trade routes in the Great Sea, the Red Sea, and the Indian Ocean.

No week passes without a camel caravan lumbering through Jericho on the way to Babylon or Egypt. Whether or not they sell their goods to our merchants, we profit from their presence. Taxes on the caravan trade are just one source of the wealth that has poured into our treasuries in the past few years.

It was to talk about those taxes that the Queen of Sheba came to visit me. And what an entourage she brought with her! Her camels were laden to the breaking point, their saddlebags bulging with spices for the palace kitchens, with gold, and with precious stones for the royal coffers. She had heard of my wealth and wisdom, and she sought to impress me with hers.

But it worked the other way. With wide-eyed wonder, she looked at my palace with its rich hangings and lavish furniture; at my tables stocked with the finest meats, the richest sauces, the choicest wines; at my court, staffed by a legion of officials and servants; at the offerings burnt to the Lord in the temple. I watched her take it all in—and then turn pale at the sight: "The report was true which I heard in my own land of your affairs and of your wisdom, but I did not believe the reports until I came and my own eyes had seen it; and, behold, the half was not told me;

your wisdom and prosperity surpass the report which I heard" (I Kings 10:6-7).

Her astonishment worked in my favor as we discussed the business agreements between our countries. Sheba, in southwest Arabia, was a great center of trade in spices and incense. But more and more I was in position to compete with, or even control, their enterprises. For one thing, the most lucrative trade was with Babylon and the other great cities of the east, and the safest caravan routes ran through my domain. Only with my permission could such business thrive. For another thing, my ships were more and more active around the Arabian peninsula. That meant that I, too, was buying and selling goods on which Sheba used to have a virtual monopoly.

A hundred and twenty talents of gold were what that treaty cost the Queen—with huge quantities of spices and gems thrown in. When she left, she had what she wanted —a peaceful trade agreement. And a wealthy king was even wealthier! When the fresh winds from the Western Sea blow through the marketplace, I can smell the reminders of her visit in the rich fragrance of the Sheban spices.

Copper vessels of fine quality and wide variety are also available in the marketplace. They too testify to my enterprise as a merchant. The metal for them was smelted at Ezion-Geber. It is not only carried by donkey and ox-cart here to Jerusalem but is shipped by my fleet to the seaports of the world. My people are not good sailors, so establishing that fleet was one of my harder chores. Happily my relationship with Hiram, king of the Phoenician port of Tyre, is such that I can count on him for sailors to man our ships. What a job they have done, carrying copper to diverse foreign ports and returning with their cargoes of gold, silver, hardwood, jewels, ivory, and varieties of apes for the amusement of our noble families.

Horse trading as well as copper smelting has become a profitable industry. My men buy strong, speedy warhorses from Cilicia and sell them to the Hittites and Aramaeans who live to the north of us. Furthermore, the Egyptians use me as an agent to sell their chariots—those light and mobile instruments of war that have transformed our military tactics in the past century—to our neighbors.

To see the difference I have made in Jerusalem we need to stroll past the palace as well as the market. It is not the architecture that I am most proud of, though it is a splendid house, worthy of the king who serves God's people. It is the administrative structure that works within that is my pride and joy. David bequeathed to me vast lands—virtually from the borders of Egypt to the banks of the Euphrates. Previous leaders—the judges, Saul, David —had more trouble than they could handle just keeping twelve spirited tribes together. And those tribes were all children of Jacob—Israel—our father. Think of the problems now. The Edomites to the south resent our authority. The Ammonites and Moabites to the east chafe under the taxes we levy. The Philistines to the west wonder when they will be strong enough to break our yoke. The Syrians, or Aramaeans, as we call them, to the north continually plot their independence.

The tasks of governing these peoples, of keeping the trade routes open, of assuring a sufficient flow of taxes and laborers to accomplish my massive building projects demand a highly efficient group of administrators. These I have gathered, and with me they have reorganized our entire political system: administrative districts have taken the place of the old tribal boundaries; sons of the tribes have been conscripted for military duty and forced labor; taxes have reached an all-time high. The price has been steep, but we have accomplished what we set out to.

I have saved the best till the last on our stroll through Jerusalem. To the east of the city I built it, with the help of Phoenician architects and artisans. There it stands proud and high on the rock—the house of the Lord God of Israel. In front of it can be seen the great bronze altar where burnt offerings send their smoke heavenward, with the prayers of the people. Thirty feet square and fifteen feet high that altar is—a massive monument to our dependence on God. Between the altar and the temple's porch is the laver, a great bronze basin, fifteen feet across, resting on the backs of four groups of oxen cast in bronze.

And then there is the temple itself, approached by graceful steps and fronted by a majestic porch on which stand two ornate pillars. Within are two vast chambers, exquisitely decorated with carved cedar paneling, inlaid with gold. The first chamber is the holy place, in which stands the golden incense altar, lifting its fragrance day and night as an expression of our devotion to God. With it are the table for showbread and five pairs of lampstands, constant reminders that only our God gives true nourishment and illumination.

The inmost chamber, the holy of holies we call it, shelters the ark of God, brought to Jerusalem by my father. Hovering over the ark are two winged cherubim, symbols of God's sovereignty over all his creation. Most important—and almost too holy to speak of—is the bright cloud that rests over the ark, the visual reassurance that the Lord who led our fathers through the wilderness by a pillar of cloud is yet with us.

If I have spared few details in my description of the temple, it is because it occupies the central place in our lives. All else that we do has as its true goal the continuation and enhancement of our worship. Our great glory is not our military might with its great regiments of chariotry, or our commercial enterprises with their sprawling network of trading treaties, or our efficient administrative structure with its host of regulations and legion of officials. Our great glory is the name of the most high God, who has deigned to choose us for himself and make his dwelling place among us.

So there they are—the market, the palace, the temple. How did I accomplish all of this? How did I change the very face of Jerusalem and grant it a beauty that David could only dream of?

For the answer to those questions I go back to the beginning of my reign. The Lord appeared to me in a dream and spoke to me only these words: "Ask what I shall give you." Weighed down with the burdens of my tasks, I knew immediately what I needed: "And now, O Lord my God, thou hast made thy servant king in place of David my father, although I am but a little child; I do not know how to go out or come in. . . . Give thy servant therefore an understanding mind to govern thy people, that I may discern between good and evil; for who is able to govern this thy great people?" (I Kings 3:5, 7, 9).

Wisdom to get work done, wisdom to make sound decisions, wisdom to judge right from wrong—wisdom to collect proverbs by which we can guide our lives—wisdom was the gift I asked for and received. God's gift, then, all of this is. To him goes the credit for those bright threads in my cord of life.

But what about the darker strands? If I had it to do over again, there are some things I would do differently.

Strangely enough, my strengths became my weaknesses; my successes led to my failures.

Wisdom was the gift God gave me. Through it my enterprises flourished, my reputation thrived. Yet at crucial points in life I played the fool. Even now the seeds of my folly are about to come to flower. Many of my people are vexed by the heavy tax load they bear and especially by the forced labor which drafts their sons away from village and field and consigns them to one of my work crews. Rehoboam, who is destined to succeed me on the throne, will have his hands full to keep down revolt.

Had I it to do over, I would settle for fewer accomplishments and more harmony among my people. Heady with my sense of achievement, driving to establish a great empire in my generation, I somehow failed to seek God's fresh guidance and instead relied on a wisdom more mine than his.

Zeal for God's name was something I cherished as firmly as the wisdom God granted me. Yet here my blunders were colossal. If I could have a second chance, my life would take a different turn. Political alliances were crucial to my plans. No empire can be built on force alone. Good will among nations allows for much greater economic success than military might. The best way—or so I thought—to build bridges of friendship was to take as wives the daughters of foreign rulers. What king would dare attack my borders if his daughter graced my harem? Politically this practice proved wise. In agreement upon agreement I took for myself the noble daughters of our neighbors: Moabites, Ammonites, Edomites, Sidonians, and Hittites. Even Pharaoh's daughter became my wife.

Politically wise yet spiritually foolish—that is how I see the matter now. These women whom I loved with a passion and tried desperately to please enticed me to compromise my zeal for the name and house of the Lord. I stagger now to think of it. Shrines and high places were built on the mountains east of here—places where my wives could worship Chemosh, god of Moab, Molech of the Ammonites, and Ashtoreth, goddess of the Sidonians. I who had built and dedicated a house for the true and living God was now building sanctuaries in wholesale fashion for pagan deities.

Wisdom turned to folly, and spiritual zeal became idolatry. I hang my head in shame at the thought. How

God will judge me and my people I dread to contemplate. Perhaps our twelve tribes will again be torn asunder, and two kingdoms will take the place of one.

Yet somehow the Lord of hosts will see his people through. His hand is at work in my accomplishments; his hand will continue to work despite my failure. As for the God of the Exodus, the conquest, and the kingdom—he will get his work done. As for me—the beauty of my achievements is overlaid by the ashes of my regret.

Chapter 17

Jehoshaphat:
King Who Trusted God

And Jehoshaphat stood in the assembly of Judah and Jerusalem, in the house of the LORD, before the new court, and said, "O Lord, GOD of our fathers, art thou not God in heaven? Dost thou not rule over all the kingdoms of the nations? In thy hand are power and might, so that none is able to withstand thee.... And now behold, the men of Ammon and Moab and Mount Seir, whom thou wouldest not let Israel invade when they came from the land of Egypt, and whom they avoided and did not destroy— O our God, wilt thou not execute judgment upon them? For we are powerless against this great multitude that is coming against us. We do not know what to do, but our eyes are upon thee."

(II Chronicles 20:5-6, 10-12.)

"We do not know what to do, but our eyes are upon thee." My prayer had ended with those words, and I had never prayed with more urgency. The whole congregation had stood with me—the bearded elders of Jerusalem, the strong warriors of Benjamin's tribe, the priests and Levites who served the temple, the sheep raisers from the hills of Tekoa, and the grape growers from south of Hebron. Palms stretched out to God, they had supported my prayer with theirs.

To pray was all we could do. The news was too dire, the need too urgent, for any other remedy. Even as we prayed, the enemy troops were marching north. Bulletin after bulletin brought word of their intent—to conquer the land of Judah, sack our capital, and sell our sons and daughters into slavery.

"We do not know what to do, but our eyes are upon thee." These were not words of mock humility or of false trust. We had no other plan for survival, and we needed no other. The prayer finished, we waited—I the king, my elders, and my countrymen from men bent and bearded to babies nestled at their mothers' breasts—we waited for a word from the Lord.

It was one of the sons of Asaph, the temple musicians who had given us so many of our psalms, that the Lord used to give us his word. Jahaziel was his name, and how the Spirit of the Lord came upon him! "Hearken, all Judah and inhabitants of Jerusalem, and King Jehoshaphat" was the way he began. And, of course, we were all ears to hear him proceed: "Thus says the Lord to you, 'Fear not, and be not dismayed at this great multitude; for the battle is not yours but God's. Tomorrow go down against them; behold, they will come up by the ascent of Ziz; you will find them at the end of the valley, east of the wilderness of Jeruel. You will not need to fight in this battle; take your position, stand still, and see the victory of the Lord on your behalf, O Judah and Jerusalem.' Fear not, and be not dismayed; tomorrow go out against them, and the Lord will be with you" (II Chronicles 20:15–17).

What a word of hope! What a promise of salvation! The Redeemer who plucked from Egypt a straggling band of slaves and planted them in Canaan to flourish like a great vine was to see to it that hostile beasts did not trample his plantings or spoil his vineyard. Our fears subsided. The Lord had shown us his will.

The multitude that assembled early the next morning to march to Tekoa's wilderness looked like no army I had ever seen. We were the strangest military regiment to take the field since Gideon moved against the Midianites armed with trumpet, torch, and pitcher. Instead of the rattling of armor, there was the lilt of song:

> "Give thanks to the Lord,
>   for his steadfast love endures for ever"
>   (II Chronicles 20:21).

As we sang, the Lord acted. He confused the troops of our enemies from the east and south so that they fought each other. It was as though our God himself had laid an ambush for them. The soldiers of Ammon and Moab turned on the Edomites of Mount Seir who should have been their allies, and then, as though driven by thirst for blood, they slaughtered each other.

Why were we sent there? Surely not to fight but to watch —and to testify to the faithfulness of Judah's God. The return trip to Jerusalem was marked by even greater joy that the outward journey. Harps and lyres and trumpets joined with our voices to praise the Lord in his house where just hours before we had gathered in such fear. "Our eyes are upon thee," we had prayed with anxiety. "Our eyes are upon thee," we now affirmed with deep gratitude and full confidence.

The news of God's victory spread among the nearby nations like fire on a summer hillside. And in its wake it left an uncanny calm like the silence after a winter storm. No king dared lift a bow against us. The swords of our neighbors rested in their scabbards. God had fought for us, and our enemies feared to quarrel with him.

This time of peace gave me the opportunity I longed for. Freedom from foreign attack strengthened my hand to deal with the greatest threats to our nationhood—the threats of idolatry and injustice at home. "Our eyes are upon thee," we had prayed in our dire emergency. But our eyes must also be on the Lord in our daily living. How could we call on his name for rescue, if we did not honor his name in our temple and our courts?

Early in my reign, I had begun a reform to bring our national life into line with our faith in the Lord God of our fathers. I refused, for instance, to seek advice from Baal and his priests, and I forbade any of my officials to participate in Baal worship. Who would have thought that a king of Judah would need to impose that kind of ban? Our whole history was a warning signal against entanglement with strange gods. The gods of Egypt were defeated in pitched battle with our God at the beginning of our history. And the gods of Canaan proved powerless against him when Joshua's troops conquered Jericho and Ai.

Yet some of the kings before me—David's sons they were in flesh but not in heart—used to seek Baal's counsel in their decisions about political or military activities. A king of Judah dependent on a Canaanite god of fertility for wisdom and insight? It was unthinkable, but it had happened—and all too regularly. God's kings had consulted Baal's magicians. Imagine them shaping their plans on the basis of the color of a fish liver or the contour of the entrails of a calf. Think of them trying to discern God's will in the shrouds of sacred smoke or in the pattern left by wine dregs in the magic cup.

All this I had banned, in my effort to obey God's commandments and to encourage my people to do likewise. The high places also needed my attention. Like barley shoots they sprang up on the hilltops of the nation. There soil was cleared and on the rocky slabs altars were built for sacrifice to the gods of Canaan—or even to the Lord of Judah. Beside the altars stood pillars of wood or stone called *asherim,* images to honor Asherah, goddess of the sea. An unspeakable blend of our covenant faith with the pagan religion of the Canaanites stained these high places. Wherever they were raised our beliefs were compromised. I had no choice but to condemn and to destroy them, though whenever my officers turned their backs the high places reappeared.

One of the worst things about those shrines was that they harbored ritual prostitution. The Canaanites believe that the fertility of the crops and flocks is dependent on human sexual activity. When men and women lie with the sacred prostitutes they encourage Baal and his mistress Anath to have intercourse. That intercourse is thought to be responsible for the spring fertility when the trees blossom and the cows drop their calves. An abominable belief this is. In the name of religion people are seduced into immorality. The marriage command is broken; the stability of the family is threatened; and the name of our God is blasphemed. Strong measures are called for, and I have had to take them despite the protests of my people.

Idolatry, sexual license, and injustice—these have been the targets of my reform. My aim has been to get the people to return to the patterns which God commanded to Moses our father. To do this, I have had to set up a crew of teachers and priests to take the law to every village and town in the hills and plains of Judah.

The knowledge of the law had to be accompanied by the enforcement of the law. The old system of justice where a few elders in the city gate made the basic decisions did not seem to work so well any more. Customs had changed, and foreign practices had been adopted. So I sent judges to the main cities—the ones I had fortified as defense against invasion. My instruction to them was simple: "Consider what you do, for you judge not for man but for the Lord; he is with you in giving judgment. Now then, let the fear of the Lord be upon you; take heed what you do, for there is no perversion of justice with the Lord our God, or partiality, or taking bribes" (II Chronicles 19:6–7). How else can we view our part as human rulers and judges? Are we not God's representatives, obliged to follow his pattern of justice as closely as possible?

Not that we can do that perfectly. That is why I also set up a court of appeal in Jerusalem. There a group of leading priests, Levites, and noblemen were appointed to hear disputed cases. Again my instructions showed how important I viewed their task to be: "Thus you shall do in the fear of the Lord, in faithfulness, and with your whole heart: whenever a case comes to you from your brethren who live in their cities, concerning bloodshed, law or commandment, statutes or ordinances, then you shall instruct them, that they may not incur guilt before the Lord and wrath may not come upon you and your brethren. . . . Deal courageously, and may the Lord be with the upright!" (II Chronicles 19:9–11).

The faith of my father David to trust God in all things, and the wisdom of my father Solomon to deal with the difficulties of a growing country—those were my wishes. How inadequate I felt for the tasks and how dependent on God for help. Whatever privileges went with kingship seemed far outweighed by its responsibilities. The opportunity was great for making huge mistakes.

I still hang my head in shame when I remember one of my mistakes. For years it had been my dream to build a large fleet like Solomon's and to see Judah's ships ply the seas, laden with copper ore and golden grain. We did not have the resources to do this alone, so I did what I never should have done—I joined with King Ahaziah of Israel, wicked though he was, in building and manning the fleet. Even after the prophet Eliezer of the town of Mareshah predicted destruction for the fleet—I blush to think of it—I still persisted. The news of the massive shipwreck was hardly unexpected. But what a waste in men, in goods, in money! And what a price to learn a lesson I should have already known.

I was there the day King Ahab of Israel had paid with his life for refusing to obey the words of God's prophet. Ahab's prophets were virtually puppets who learned what the king wanted and then gave him prophecies that supported his will. Micaiah was not one of them. When I called on him to give Ahab and me the word of the Lord concerning our campaign in Ramoth-Gilead, he saw "all Israel scattered upon the mountains as sheep that have no shepherd"—an obvious reference to the death of a king who leaves his people leaderless. Yet Ahab marched his men anyhow and took an arrow from a Syrian archer between the joints of his armor.

In the mercy of God I escaped, more convinced than ever that in all things I had to trust and obey him. Now after a quarter century of ruling, the time of my departure has come.

Behind me I shall leave a well-fortified country, a well-equipped army, a well-managed political and judicial system. Behind me I shall leave a covenant faith fairly well purged of pagan compromise. Behind me I shall leave memories of massive battles fought and won in the strength of the Lord.

But my greatest legacy may be a simple prayer, a prayer which tells how important trust in God really is and how great my trust really was:

"We do not know what to do, but our eyes are upon thee."

Chapter 18

Elijah:
Prophet of the
Great Covenant

And at the time of the offering of the oblation, Elijah the prophet came near and said, "O LORD, God of Abraham, Isaac, and Israel, let it be known this day that thou art God in Israel, and that I am thy servant, and that I have done all these things at thy word. Answer me, O LORD, answer me, that this people may know that thou, O LORD, art God, and that thou hast turned their hearts back." Then the fire of the LORD fell, and consumed the burnt offering, and the wood, and the stones, and the dust, and licked up the water that was in the trench. And when all the people saw it, they fell on their faces; and they said, "The LORD, he is God; the LORD, he is God." And Elijah said to them, "Seize the prophets of Baal; let not one of them escape." And they seized them; and Elijah brought them down to the brook Kishon, and killed them there.

(I Kings 18:36–40.)

My eyes filled with hope as I looked at the younger prophet. The work that I had given my life to would go on. God would see to that. And Elisha stood ready to be his servant.

I did not envy the young man or long to trade places with him. The battles had been hard. My face and frame showed the marks of decades of struggle. My foes had been formidable—the prophets of Baal, the wealthy gentry, the kings and queens of Israel. Tooth and claw they had fought me, and the long savage fight had taken its toll. I was ready to rest, ready to go to my fathers and sleep in peace.

My wish for Elisha was a simple one: may he continue to let Israel know that the Lord is the true and living God, the only rightful King. Just there was the center of my struggles—the kings of Israel, Ahab and Ahaziah, had contested God's right to be King. He, of course, had won each contest, but how much blood—how much needless blood—was shed along the way.

Can I say that the battle has been won once for all? No, I cannot. Such spiritual battles have to be waged in every generation. We always live on the edge of paganism. Idolatry, immorality, injustice—the great threats to our faith—are ever only a step away. Elisha knows this, and he also knows that we have no weapons with which to win this fight but the might of God's Holy Spirit. It was this combination—an eager young prophet and a mighty God—that filled my eyes with hope as we stood on Jordan's east bank, Elisha and I, and waited for the end to come.

At the beginning of my ministry I had learned that the Lord was Israel's true King. Impelled by a powerful word from God, I had to face Ahab in his palace at Samaria. The word I delivered had nearly cost me my life: "As the Lord the God of Israel lives, before whom I stand, there shall be neither dew nor rain these years, except by my word" (I Kings 17:1).

What angered King Ahab was not only the prospect of lengthy drought with its inevitable famine, but even more the insult to his religious practices that my prophecy conveyed. What I was saying was this: "My word as a true prophet of Israel is more powerful than all the prayers,

all the magic, all the rituals of your prophets of Baal." Or
even more bluntly: "I as God's humble servant from the
plains of Gilead have more control over Israel's destiny
than you do as a lofty king in an ivory palace."

I had to run for my life. Happy I was when God told
me to flee across the Jordan to the brook Cherith—happy
because it was not far from my family home of Tishbe in
the region of Gilead and happy because I knew the brook
Cherith would continue to run with water after most of
Israel's streams had dried up.

But after a while my prophecy caught up with me as
well. The brook, which slaked my thirst while the God-
sent ravens brought my bread, dried up. Again God's
word made clear my next move. To the far north and west
I was to journey—to Zarephath on the Great Sea. North I
walked along the bluffs of the Jordan, then west and
north through the Valley of Jezreel where the ghosts of a
hundred wars linger among the hills. Under the lee of Mt.
Carmel I reached the coastal plain and saw for the first
time the bright blue furrows of the Western Sea. Then it
was north again about three days' journey past the stately
towers and lofty sails of Tyre and its merchant fleet to
Zarephath just ten miles from Sidon.

Only the word of God could have sent me there. My
rustic home in Tishbe seemed worlds away from this
Phoenician town. My faith was made firm as a stone
foundation when I reached the gates of the town. There a
widow gathered sticks for her fire, and there God confirmed to me that this was the woman with whom I was
to lodge. All that distance from home, far from Israel's
boundaries, in this other world of merchants, ships, and
sailors, the Lord God of our fathers provided for me a
home.

What a God he is! He put down a powerful king by
withholding rain from his realm, yet he supplied boundless amounts of meal and oil for a widow in a foreign
country. He plotted against the priests and prophets of
Samaria, while he raised from the dead the son of an
obscure Gentile woman. He was the God of the people
with whom he had made covenant, but he judged his own
people forcefully while he tenderly blessed those who did
not yet know his name. Young Elisha will find this out,
too, when the prophet's mantle falls on him.

How different the compassion of the true King from

the greed of Ahab the impostor, who thought ivory couch-
es and golden vessels were the marks of royalty. The
justice and love which are the garments of kingship were
not part of Ahab's wardrobe. He wore instead the rags
of avarice and lust.

I saw this especially in his grasping scheme to rob
Naboth of his vineyard. With flagrant disregard of Israel's
ancient customs he tried, first by charm and then by force,
to defraud Naboth of the land inherited from his fathers.
The land in question lay close to the palace in Samaria,
and Ahab thought it would be an excellent plot for a
vegetable garden. And indeed it would have, because for
generations it had been lovingly tilled, tended, and cul-
tivated. Its neat rows of vines produced grapes as fine as
any in the region. Naboth cared for the land and its plantings as he would for his own child.

In a sense, we Israelites viewed our land as part of our
family. We did not trade it or sell it except in dire circumstances. It was part of the inheritance God had given
our fathers under Joshua, and for three centuries and
more we had clung to it and lived off it—generation after
generation.

Why Ahab refused to understand this, I do not know.
His greed was boundless; his admiration of his own power
knew no limits. And there was Jezebel to spur him on.
She was not one of us in birth, religion, or spirit. She was
as brutal and heartless as the pagan faith in which she was
raised and which she had planted like wheat in every plain
and valley of Israel. Her upbringing in the palace of
Sidon had taught her ways of royalty that were utterly
foreign to us.

Our kings were thought to be servants, called to help us
obey the will of God as determined in his law. Their kings
were masters, puffed up with their own power. The Sidonians—like the other Phoenicians—even thought that their
kings were divine, elevated to deity by the blessing of the
gods. What they wanted to do, they did. The laws of their
lands were shaped by their whims.

Jezebel it was who prodded Ahab to seize Naboth's vineyard at any price. The ultimate price was too horrible to
contemplate—the savage murder of a humble Israelite
farmer. The king's lust for power was sated for the time,
but his greed had signed his own death warrant. Years later,
when the Syrian archer sped his arrow between the joints

of Ahab's armor, my dire prophecy was fulfilled: "In the place where dogs licked up the blood of Naboth shall dogs lick your own blood" (I Kings 21:19).

The God of the covenant had judged the king for his violation of the terms of the covenant. The King above all kings had shown how righteous he is and what righteousness he requires, especially of those whom men call kings. I looked at young Elisha full of hope, because it was that King who had anointed him for service.

Contesting with kings, it seemed, had become a way of life for me. There was the time just recently that Ahab's son Ahaziah was seriously wounded as he fell through the lattice that screened a window in his upper chamber. Why he fell no one has said. My guess is that he was in a drunken stupor to escape the turmoil which shook the throne of Israel after Ahab's death.

Insult was added to injury when he tried to determine the outcome of his illness. Would he recover from his wounds? A good question that, but he should have asked a prophet of the true and living God. Instead he sent messengers south to Ekron in the territory of the Philistines to inquire about his fate of Baalzebul, the pagan god of that region. His very name was accursed by us. We did not call him Baalzebul, "Lord of the high place"; we called him Baal-zebub, "Lord of the flies."

At God's command I intercepted the king's messengers and sent them back to Samaria with the grim assurance that their king's illness was fatal. Twice the smitten king sent emissaries to beg me to reverse my prediction (or perhaps to destroy me so that my word would perish with me), and God struck both groups dead.

The God of the covenant alone was Lord of the future. His hand held the reins of history. Any attempt by king or deity to usurp his lordship was met by drastic action. That memory fed my confidence as I looked at Elisha, my spiritual son, and prepared to leave my ministry to him.

The Lord of the covenant, Master of foreign worlds, Shepherd of needy widows, Judge of all unrighteous, Guardian of the future—this is the God whom I have served. None other is worthy.

As I voice these thoughts, my heart flies to the top of Mt. Carmel. I see myself standing there again. To the north stretches the narrow coastal plains to Tyre, Sidon, and beyond. To the south more coastline and just over the hazy horizon the cities of the Philistines. To the east the sweeping valley of Jezreel with its pastured slopes that climb to the massive hills of Galilee; and to the west the endless reaches of the Great Sea where dwell the sons of Caphtor and Javan.

With all the world within my view, I stood alone—yet not alone. The time had come to put the faith of our fathers to the test.

Arrayed against me were the prophets of Baal and Asherah, lackeys of Ahab and Jezebel, sponsored by their court, nourished in their palaces. By the hundreds they had come to pit their faith against mine.

The contest was a simple one. An altar was built. A bull was slain, cut into pieces, and placed on the altar. The wood was stacked against the altar, but no fire was lit.

That was the test. Who could send fire? From morning till well beyond noon the prophets of the gods of Canaan wailed their loud supplications, chanted their magic spells, performed their bloody rituals, cutting themselves with swords and lances.

No fire came. The slaughtered bull began to stink. The wood lay dry and silent. I could not resist a taunt: "Cry aloud, for he is a god; either he is musing, or he has gone aside, or he is on a journey, or perhaps he is asleep and must be awakened" (I Kings 18:27). But there was no answer; there was no fire.

Defeated, done in, disheartened, they stood by while I built my altar, slaughtered my bull, stacked my wood. Confident in the God of the covenant, I dug trenches around the altar. Then I soaked the bull and the wood with water until the trenches filled.

My prayer was brief. No weeping and wailing, no gashing of my flesh. Just the direct request: "Let it be known this day that thou art God in Israel, and that I am thy servant, and that I have done all these things at thy word" (I Kings 18:36). As I finished my prayer, on edge with anticipation, the fire of the Lord fell.

The crucial point had been made; the contest had been won. The Lord could then end the drought with which my ministry had begun. A cloud the size of a human hand signalled the coming of the storms. Having shown his might by fire, the covenant Lord was ready to show his mercy by rain.

That unique Lord, before whom all rivals had to crumble, is now ready to receive me. No easy days lie ahead for Elisha, but hope wells within me. The God of the fire and rain, the God of the ravens and the widows, will see his prophets through.

Chapter 19

Elisha:
Prophet of
Compassionate Power

When Elisha came into the house, he saw the child lying dead on his bed. So he went in and shut the door upon the two of them, and prayed to the LORD. Then he went up and lay upon the child, putting his mouth upon his mouth, his eyes upon his eyes, and his hands upon his hands; and as he stretched himself upon him, the flesh of the child became warm. Then he got up again, and walked once to and fro in the house, and went up, and stretched himself upon him; the child sneezed seven times, and the child opened his eyes. Then he summoned Gehazi and said, "Call this Shunammite." So he called her. And when she came to him, he said, "Take up your son." She came and fell at his feet, bowing to the ground; then she took up her son and went out.

(II Kings 4:32–37.)

The words fell dimly on my ears at first. As Joash, Israel's king, repeated them, I stirred to consciousness. For days my life had been spent in that dull twilight between sleep and wakefulness. Restless with fever, frozen with chills, I tossed on my narrow cot and watched the wick of life burn low.

It was the familiar voice of the king that snatched me awake. That familiar voice and the even more familiar words: "My father, my father! The chariots of Israel and its horsemen!" (II Kings 13:14). We gazed at each other through eyes hazy with tears, the king and I. His were tears of sadness at the pending loss of a friend; mine were tears of memory, as I recalled another time when I had heard those words.

Even in my weakness, the sights and the sounds of that memory stood sharply before me. It was a day that no one could forget. I had followed Elijah to the Jordan and across. Even the crossing was memorable. The old prophet took his mantle from his shoulders, rolled it into a rodlike bundle, and struck the waters with it. Like Joshua before us, we walked to the eastern bank on dry land.

For a moment we stood engrossed in conversation. I had asked him to grant me a double portion of his spirit so that I could carry out the responsibilities that were to fall on me. "A hard thing," he had called my request, because only God could give the answer. Yet true prophet that he was, Elijah set up a sign by which God would grant or refuse my request: "... if you see me as I am being taken from you, it shall be so for you; but if you do not see me, it shall not be so" (II Kings 2:10).

I did not have to wait long for the sign. Even while Elijah and I were talking, a chariot of fire and horses of fire took Elijah from my side. And a mighty force, like a whirlwind, lifted him to heaven before my very eyes. In shocked despair I cried after him, "My father, my father! The chariots of Israel and its horsemen!" (II Kings 2:12). Then I saw him no more.

For minutes I stood in stunned confusion. Since that day so many years ago when Elijah called me from my plowing—Ahab was still king then—I had walked and worked and slept by the prophet's side. I had known how much Israel's well-being had depended on his word. Now he was gone. My spiritual father was gone. And Israel's strength—worth more than her chariots and horsemen—was gone.

Who could possibly take his place? I pondered. Then it began to dawn on me. I had seen him depart. The sign had pointed to me. At my feet lay Elijah's mantle, blown from his shoulders by the whirlwind. Eagerly, yet anxiously, I rolled it up and ran to the edge of the Jordan. As I struck the water with it, I shouted, "Where is the Lord, the God of Elijah?" (II Kings 2:14). The parted river and its dry bed confirmed my call: I had been granted the grace to see the prophet carried to heaven; his mantle had fallen on me; and Elijah's God had heard my cry. As Joshua knew for certain that he was to take Moses' place, so I felt God's touch on my shoulder, pushing me to fulfill Elijah's ministry—and with a double portion of his spirit, a *double* portion like the inheritance of a first-born son.

"My father, my father. The chariots of Israel and its horsemen!" That had been my lament more than forty years before. Now young Joash, who had so often looked to me for God's counsel, was weeping that same dirge over me.

I knew why he was weeping. Even as I lay quiet, waiting for the Lord to take me in death, the Syrians were readying their equipment and mustering their troops to do battle with Israel. Without the Lord's help, Joash's men had little chance. Weak as I was, the Lord prompted me to help him.

"Take a bow and arrows," I ordered. "Open the window eastward and shoot." As Joash drew the bow taut, I shouted, "The Lord's arrow of victory, the arrow of victory over Syria!" Then I told the king to take the arrows and strike the ground with them. Three times he struck the ground—only three times. I was chagrined: "You should have struck five or six times; then you would have struck down Syria until you had made an end of it, but now you will strike down Syria only three times" (II Kings 13:19).

Would that Joash had the faith of the widow whom I met early in my ministry. Her husband had been a member of the band of prophets—"sons of the prophets," we called them—with whom Elijah and I were connected. Deeply in debt, she feared the creditor who threatened to take her two children as slaves if she could not pay her debts. Moved by her plight, as Elijah had been in his stay with the widow of Zarephath, I trusted God to meet her need. All she had was a jar of oil. The rest was up to the Lord.

"Go outside," I had urged her, "borrow vessels of all your neighbors and not too few." Then I told her to start filling the vessels from the jar of oil. Vessel after vessel she had filled, until all the borrowed vessels brimmed with oil. Only then did her original jar empty itself. She had shown her faith by borrowing as many vessels as possible. The oil was sold; the debts were paid; the children were saved.

"My father, my father! The chariots of Israel and its horsemen!" These words of Joash did describe the part that I had played in the life of the people. The counsel that God gave me was more important to Israel's kings than prancing steeds or shining spears.

There was the time, for instance, that Jehoram of Israel and Jehoshaphat of Judah summoned me for counsel, as they marched against Mesha, king of Moab. Ahab had just died, and Mesha tried to take advantage of the change of government to gain his independence from Israel. The tribute he had to pay yearly to Ahab was keeping his people in poverty—100,000 lambs and the wool of 100,000 rams.

With the king of Edom as a reluctant ally—he was obligated to do Jehoshaphat's bidding—the other two kings wound their way through terrain so desolate that no water was found for either the soldiers or the donkeys that carried their gear. Anxious lest their expedition fail, they sent for me to find out God's will.

At first I refused to give Jehoram any help. Why did he not call on the prophets of Baal and Asherah like Ahab his father and Jezebel his mother? But he protested that it was Israel's Lord God who had sent them marching and it was *his* will that the kings sought. About Jehoshaphat I had no doubts. His stalwart faith and firm obedience I knew well. For his sake I sought God's message.

The immediate need was water. The Lord's first word was directed to that problem: "Thus says the Lord, 'I will make this dry streambed full of pools'" (II Kings 3:16). But beyond the need for water lay the dread of battle: "This [that is, the water] is a light thing in the sight of the Lord; he will also give the Moabites into your hand,

and you shall conquer every fortified city, and every choice
city, and shall fell every good tree, and stop up all springs
of water, and ruin every good piece of land with stones"
(II Kings 3:18-19).

There was the promise. Jehoram and Jehoshaphat had
learned what they needed. God would prosper their arms
against Moab.

Special insight and special protection were two of God's
great gifts to me. I knew that as long as he had sent me
to do his will he would provide for me full protection.
How dramatically this was made clear when the king of
Syria ordered his men against me.

The king's anger had boiled over like a pot of lentils
on a high fire. Several times he had tried to surprise our
own king with bands of raiders. Each time the Lord warned
me beforehand and I, in turn, warned the king. The Syrian
king was furious and accused his own palace guard of
treachery, until someone told him about me: "Elisha, the
prophet who is in Israel, tells the king of Israel the words
that you speak in your bedchamber" (II Kings 6:12).

To Dothan, where I was staying, the Syrian troops
marched, surrounding the town. My servant was terrified
at the sight until I asked God to open his eyes. What he
saw filled his heart with trust: the mountain was covered
with horses and fiery chariots that surrounded me. The
God who had convoyed my spiritual father Elijah to
heaven had sent his fiery hosts to guard me.

"The chariots of Israel and its horsemen"—that is what
Joash called me. Prophets were like that. Our special relationship to God gives us special power. Not that we
could take any credit for it. But it allowed us to demon-
strate God's compassion on the suffering and the afflicted.

My breath was short and my sight was dim. But one
face my memory recalled with the sharpness of a mountain crag against the setting sun. It was a noble face, the
face of a leader confident of his abilities, comfortable in his
station. The face was Syrian, not Israelite.

When I first met Naaman, the commander of the Syrian
army, he had just come south from Damascus to beg
help of Israel's king. Not military help did he need. Chariots he had aplenty and gold to buy more. What he needed
could not be bought. He was a leper. That was why the
king of Israel needed my help. Naaman had come to him.

Yet he was both powerless to help and anxious lest Naaman hate him for not helping.

But God had shown me the cure for Naaman's ailment: "Go and wash in the Jordan seven times, and your flesh shall be restored, and you shall be clean" (II Kings 5:10). Naaman protested at first, but finally went to the Jordan. He had no choice. His leprosy had him in despair, and no other hope for cure was at hand. What a sight he was when he came up from the Jordan—skin pink and shiny like a baby's. God's was the power, not mine. And nothing proved that more convincingly than a miracle worked when I was not even present.

"The chariots of Israel and its horsemen." Yes, I had been used of God to protect and provide for his people. But God did not need me. When he took Moses, Joshua was at hand. When he took David, Solomon ruled in wisdom. When he took Elijah, he poured out Elijah's spirit on me—and in double measure. And as my time comes, his care for his people will go on.

True, I as a prophet did what I could in counseling kings, in rebuking rebels, in caring for the poor, in showing compassion to the needy, in predicting the course of Israel's future. But the power to do this was God's; the lessons to be learned were his; the compassion I demonstrated I had first seen in him.

"The chariots of Israel and its horsemen." Yes, I shall be remembered for words of fierce indignation and deeds of strong power. But more than anything else I would like to be remembered as one who brought God's love to those whose hearts were broken.

Through eyes dulled by the passing of the years I can hear again the gentle voice of the Shunammite woman with whom I used to stay. Tenderly she begged God to give her a son. Her plea moved me deeply, and I assured her that God would bless her womb, even though her husband was an aged man.

Even more clearly can I hear her voice sobbing at my feet in bitter distress at the death of her only son. Her plight spurred me to pray as fervently as at any time in my life. As I stretched myself over the body of the dead boy, I begged God to stir him with life. Twice I did this, and then I felt the boy move. His sound was the most welcomed music of my life—a sneeze.

The God of compassionate power had shown his love for a young child. That thought comforts me now. Joash may have called me "the chariots of Israel and its horsemen." But as my strength slips away I feel more like a little child, weak and helpless, yet sure of my father's love.

Chapter 20

Hezekiah:
King of Zealous Obedience

In the third year of Hoshea son of Elah, king of Israel, Hezekiah the son of Ahaz, king of Judah, began to reign. He was twenty-five years old when he began to reign, and he reigned twenty-nine years in Jerusalem. His mother's name was Abi the daughter of Zechariah. And he did what was right in the eyes of the LORD, according to all that David his father had done. He removed the high places, and broke the pillars, and cut down the Asherah. And he broke in pieces the bronze serpent that Moses had made, for until those days the people of Israel had burned incense to it; it was called Nehushtan. He trusted in the LORD the God of Israel; so that there was none like him among all the kings of Judah after him, nor among those who were before him. For he held fast to the LORD; he did not depart from following him, but kept the commandments which the LORD commanded Moses.

(II Kings 18:1-6.)

I could scarcely believe the reports. The Assyrian army had been wiped out. The siege of Jerusalem had been lifted by the hand of God himself. Isaiah's prophecy had come true—and in a fashion more dramatic than I had dared believe.

The prophecy itself was startling, considering the circumstances. Here we were surrounded by Sennacherib's army as a bird would be trapped in a cage. From northern Syria and southern Philistia, from Babylon and Tyre reports had come of Sennacherib's ravages. How could we help but be next?

I looked at the familiar towers of Jerusalem and imagined them leveled. In my heart I saw the temple of Solomon in shambles, with dark clouds of smoke drifting from its once proud pillars. When I closed my eyes I pictured long lines of captives filing out of the city, carrying nothing but an exile's pack. They were headed for Assyria and slavery.

Then came Isaiah's prophecy: "Therefore thus says the Lord concerning the king of Assyria, He shall not come into this city or shoot an arrow there, or come before it with a shield or cast up a siege mound against it. By the way that he came, by the same he shall return, and he shall not come into this city, says the Lord. For I will defend this city to save it, for my own sake and for the sake of my servant David" (II Kings 19:32–34).

Jerusalem had been spared. The Assyrian army lay dead on the hills and in the valleys around us. For the first time in years we had some relief from the yoke of tax and tribute that the Assyrians had imposed on the nations that they dominated.

All through my life and the reign of my father, Ahaz, we had lived in dread of their fierce armies. Year after year they had marched west after the spring rains. They fed their horses on our standing crops; their men, on our garnered grains. No treasure was safe from their greed; no woman, from their lust.

They bent our backs in oppression. Twenty-one years now had passed since they devastated Samaria and brought the northern kingdom of Israel tumbling to its knees.

Sargon, Sennacherib's father, led the Assyrians at that time. Though more than two decades have passed, the cities of the northern tribes are still licking their wounds. Their finest young men and women, especially those educated in business or government and those skilled in the crafts, were marched to Assyria and resettled there. At the same time, the king of Assyria brought people from places like Babylon and Hamath to live among and intermarry with the men and women of Israel.

The Assyrian aims were obvious: they wanted to rob the land of its leadership and to compromise its religion by contact with other religions, so that the people would have neither the ability nor the will to revolt. And as a bonus, the Assyrians gained a highly skilled work force with which to manage the empire and build its sprawling cities.

That same fate had seemed inevitable to us in Judah until the Lord told Isaiah differently. I had resisted Assyrian pressures as much as I could through the years because I had seen what they did to my father. True, I did pay tribute when I had to, but I did so mainly to buy time.

There was no way that we could defy Assyria on our own. I had to keep a sharp eye on the political scenes in Egypt and Babylonia. Perched precariously as we were in Palestine on that land bridge between the ancient valleys of the Nile and the Tigris-Euphrates, we had to look in both directions at once to keep from being pushed off by one side or the other. During my reign, the political advisers whose counsel I leaned on were divided as to who could help us most, Babylon or Egypt. I myself was caught in between, leaning one way and then the other.

What was important to me was to maintain independence sufficient to carry out my spiritual reforms. Here I had learned from my father's poor example.

Ahaz, though he had many admirable qualities, had been so twisted by Assyrian pressures that he compromised his convictions at some crucial points. My chief aim had been to correct his mistakes and to avoid making similar ones.

God's hand was heavy on Ahaz. And—I regret to say it—it had to be. My father, early in his reign, found himself swept away by the pagan practices of our neighbors. Like the kings of Samaria who usually mixed the worship of our Lord with the rites and rituals of Canaanite religion, Ahaz allowed Baal worship in the towns of Judah. Worse still, he allowed—and even practiced— child sacrifice in his devotion to the pagan gods.

Ironically, it was Israel to the north, a nation even more rebellious than Judah, that God used to judge my father. South they marched with great ferocity. Like lions they tore at the towns of Judah. And when the hunt was over, they had carried to their lairs in the north two hundred thousand captives and much spoil.

To his earlier mistakes my father added another that was worse. He courted Assyrian favor to help him resist further invasions from the Edomites and Philistines who clustered like jackals around the carcass the lions had slain.

All his appeal to Assyria had done was to expose his weaknesses. Tiglathpileser, Assyrian king at the time, sent his troops like vultures to pick the bones of Judah which the jackals had not yet cleaned.

At that point the vexed king panicked. In a vain effort to find help for his beleaguered Judah, he frantically built altars and high places all over the land and sacrificed to the gods of many places, including the gods of Damascus where Tiglathpileser had suffered defeat. Any port in the storm, any crutch when you are crippled, seems to have been Ahaz's motto.

Passionately the prophet Isaiah pleaded with my father to trust God rather than tribute or treaties or altars. It was to no avail.

But there is no need to labor this further. My aim is not to rehearse the sins of my father, but to show why my policies toward Assyria have been somewhat different. Prudent I have tried to be, without groveling before Assyrian kings and Assyrian gods as did my father.

If I have tried to be moderate in my political posture, I have also tried to be zealous in my religious practices. Looking back over the history of my people since the time of David, who founded our dynasty, a conclusion has become clear to me: the strength of our religious vitality depends on the practice of the king. Where kings have fervently guarded and promoted our covenant faith, it has flourished throughout the land. Think of David and Jehoshaphat, and Uzziah, to some extent. Where the kings have wandered from the words of God and the traditions of our fathers, the people have followed in their steps. Just as we say "Like father, like son," so we can say "Like king, like people."

My bent was to do God's will. Especially was I goaded
in my zeal toward the Lord God of Abraham and Moses
by the fall of Samaria. I had no doubt about the reasons
for that fall. The great prophets had said it would come.
A few years before I was born, Amos had gone north from
our village of Tekoa where he raised sheep and had de-
nounced the king and leaders of Israel for failing to obey
God's commands. Twenty years later, when I was a lad,
Hosea had called Israel a harlot because she had betrayed
her marriage to the Lord and had given her love to the
Baals and other false gods.

For all of this, Samaria fell. And had Judah continued
in the path set by my father, she would have fallen too.
Our holy God is not embarrassed to punish even his own
people when they stray from him. In fact, as Isaiah has
made clear to me, those closest to God have more responsibility to follow him than others. Of those who have
been most blessed he expects the most response.

So I went at my task of reforming our laws and our
worship with great intensity. Like an arrow from a strong
bow, I went at the targets which sought attention. First,
the house of the Lord needed repair. My father had all
but stripped it, both to pay tribute to Assyria and to build
his heathen altars. Then I tore down all the pagan shrines
in Jerusalem and throughout Judah. Every high place
where pagan sacrifice and ritual prostitution were practiced was smashed and cursed. Altars were toppled and
the idolatrous pillars were chopped down. Finally, the
great feasts of our past were reinstated, especially Passover.
What a reminder of our heritage that was, as we com-
memorated God's rescue from Egypt. And what a comfort
in the present when we stood in constant need of rescue—
especially from the Assyrians.

To guide us in our worship we used the psalms of David.
What sheer delight to hear the ancient temple—now nearly
250 years old—ring with the praises of God. And the
proverbs of Solomon I had my men restudy and copy for
my leaders. What a wealth of wisdom that great king collected for the people. Who can guess what troubles we
would have been spared if we had not neglected our worship and our learning?

Through all these endeavors Isaiah has been at my side
just as he is now. Every king needs his prophet. As Nathan
both rebuked and helped our father David, so Isaiah has

been for me a staff of support and a rod of correction. How blinded our perspective can become, how distorted our values, how selfish our power, unless beside us is a person through whom God speaks his clear and mighty words.

I think of that time nearly fifteen years ago when I lay sick unto death. It was Isaiah who assured me that God would hear my prayer for longer life. It was Isaiah's prayer that turned the shadow on the sundial back ten steps as a sign—an unexplainable miracle—that God would raise me up.

And it was Isaiah who had rebuked me for showing Merodachbaladan, the king of Babylon, the treasure of our temple. In my zeal to impress the king and to seek his support in my plan to declare independence from Assyria, I made the mistake of displaying our wealth. Isaiah prophesied that in due season the Babylonians would return to loot our treasuries. My sense of political expediency had once again waged war with the old prophet's insistence that Judah's security was to be found neither in Egypt nor Babylon.

This certainly proved true a couple of years ago when Sennacherib marched west to consolidate his power. New to the throne, he wanted to quell any possible revolt as soon as possible. Like evening wolves his troops prowled their way through Syria, Phoenicia, Philistia to the borders of Egypt. Then they swept north through Judah. Forty-six cities and towns they devoured. And two hundred thousand of our people they carried home as prey. Neither Babylon nor Egypt was able to intervene.

No city stood before the Assyrians. With battering rams they leveled our gates. With mounds of earth they stormed our walls. Huge slings flung massive stones at our soldiers. Eager sappers like rabbits tunneled under our fortresses. Shielded chariots wheeled from position to position, freeing the archers and spearmen to hit their targets.

When Lachish, our fortress city to the south, fell, I thought we were done for. But I had not reckoned on Isaiah. Even when Sennacherib sent three high officials to negotiate our surrender, Isaiah stood firmly with me. I prayed with more fervor than I had, even in my deadly illness: "So now, O Lord our God, save us, I beseech thee, from his hand, that all the kingdoms of the earth may know that thou, O Lord, art God alone" (II Kings 19:19).

Then it was that Isaiah spoke with such power and confidence. God's own words to the Assyrian were what he spoke:

> "But I know your sitting down
>   and your going out and coming in,
>   and your raging against me.
> Because you have raged against me
>   and your arrogance has come into
>   my ears,
> I will put my hook in your nose
>   and my bit in your mouth,
> and I will turn you back on the way
>   by which you came." (II Kings 19:27–28)

When the prophecy was uttered, the history was assured. That is the way our God works. The morning's report of Sennacherib's disaster is just the confirmation of what we already knew. Today we will shout with more confidence than ever,

> "O sing to the Lord a new song,
>   for he has done marvelous things!
> His right hand and his holy arm
>   have gotten him victory." (Psalm 98:1)

Chapter 21

Josiah:
King of Courageous Reform

Then the king sent, and all the elders of Judah and Jerusalem were gathered to him. And the king went up to the house of the LORD, and with him all the men of Judah and all the inhabitants of Jerusalem, and the priests and the prophets, all the people, both small and great; and he read in their hearing all the words of the book of the covenant which had been found in the house of the LORD. And the king stood by the pillar and made a covenant before the LORD, to walk after the LORD and to keep his commandments and his testimonies and his statutes, with all his heart and all his soul, to perform the words of this covenant that were written in this book; and all the people joined in the covenant.

(II Kings 23:1–3.)

With each bounce of the chariot my anxiety seemed to rise. The journey from Jerusalem north to Megiddo felt longer than usual, and not nearly so enjoyable. On most such journeys my eyes devoured the scenery—rugged hills that served as natural fortifications for Jerusalem, old towns that sheltered a thousand stories from our sacred past, joyful people that welcomed a king who had enlarged their freedom.

But on this journey, my heart was seized with other pictures. I imagined the strong chariotry of Necho edging north along the coastal road. Reports of the high-stepping steeds and the hard-marching troops had already reached me from my towns along the Philistine border. The Egyptians were always formidable enemies. Then I pictured my own forces—a young new army, untested by battle. Our long years of cowering before the Assyrian lion had given us no opportunity to sharpen our own claws.

Worst of all, I thought of the actual battle. Which way would it turn? Would the element of surprise and the advantage of our own terrain overcome the Egyptian superiority in numbers and experience? In a way I dreaded the encounter. My best hope was that the appearance of my men blocking the pass at Megiddo would discourage Necho into reversing his plans and returning to his palace on the Nile. My sharpest fear was that I would lose both the battle and my army, leaving the way clear for Egypt and Assyria to link arms and crush us in their fierce embrace.

The whole aim of my foreign policy had been to prevent that. For fifty years and more before I took the throne, Judah had danced to Assyria's tunes. Nineveh set the fashions for Jerusalem, whether in dress, diplomacy, morality, or religion. Miserable years they had been, as—shameful to say—my grandfather Manasseh took us to depths of degradation beneath anything that Samaria had known before her fall, more than a century ago.

Then three years ago it happened. A coalition of Scythians from the northern plains, Medes from the eastern mountains, and Babylonians from the southern valley assaulted the walls and gates of Nineveh and brought her to her knees. Jerusalem was ablaze with celebration. Not since

Sennacherib's army was destroyed by plague at her gates,
had the dwellers of the old city danced in the streets.

Nahum's strong prophecy had come to pass:

> "Woe to the bloody city,
>   all full of lies and booty—
>   no end to the plunder!
> The crack of whip, and rumble of wheel,
>   galloping horse and bounding
>   chariot!
> Horsemen charging,
>   flashing sword and glittering spear,
> hosts of slain,
>   heaps of corpses,
> dead bodies without end—
>   they stumble over the bodies!
> And all for the countless harlotries of
>   the harlot,
>   graceful and of deadly charms,
> who betrays nations with her
>   harlotries,
>   and peoples with her charms." (Nahum 3:1–4)

Reports of Nineveh's collapse brought applause in a dozen
capitals of the nations who had been betrayed by her
charms.

From the earliest years of my reign—and I came to the
throne as a lad of eight—I had longed for the day when
Judah could be free. As the Assyrian eagle was plucked by
the attacks of her neighbors, we in the west were able stage
by stage to snatch our independence.

It was my resolve to let nothing—not even the Egyptian
army—fix a yoke of slavery on our neck again.

I had my plan, and Necho had his. I was sure of this as
my chariot jostled up the last hill that offered me a dazzling
view of the valley of Jezreel and the pass at Megiddo which
guarded its western end. If Necho could cut through the
valley he could save days on his journey north and west to
Harran. His hope was to help the Assyrian king Ashur-
uballit recapture Harran and use it as a base to withstand
the conquests of the Babylonians.

Not that Necho had any love for the Assyrians. He preferred to deal with a fading Assyrian kingdom rather than
to face a Babylonian state on the rise. For my part, I had

chosen to do all that I could to keep Ashur-uballit's tattered empire from regaining its strength. What Babylon would ultimately do, I did not know. What Assyria would do if she recovered from her wounds, I did know. A whole century of our history had been scarred by her ravages.

The risks had all been weighed. No report from either the Nile or the Euphrates had changed my mind. And no word from the Lord had come to block my plans. So it was onward to the pass at Megiddo to meet my men and work my plan.

What I have said so far sounds coldly political. It is much more than that, however. My push for political freedom was part of my drive for spiritual reform.

The really high tax that the Assyrians had exacted of us was not the gold, the wine, the grain, the olive oil that we paid them yearly. It was the price of our spiritual heritage, our covenant faith, that cost us most.

A person wandering through the streets and squares of Jerusalem during the lengthy reign of Manasseh or the two short years of my father, Amon, might not have suspected that he was in Judah at all. The pagan altars, the shrines where the sun and stars were worshipped, the wizards, soothsayers, and mediums in the marketplace, the male prostitutes in the temple courtyards—all of these made Jerusalem look like Tyre or Gaza or Damascus in its paganness.

All that our people stood for in our special relationship with God was washing away in the tides of Manasseh's marriage to Assyria. We trusted foreign alliances for our security, as if there had been no exodus from Egypt. We followed foreign examples of morality, as if there had been no law at Sinai. We practiced foreign modes of religion, as if there had never been a tabernacle of Aaron or a temple of Solomon.

It was to lift that shame, to blot out that evil that I was riding north and urging my driver to chide the horses forward. At Megiddo I would change chariots and garments. Necho's men could desire nothing more than to rout my troops by killing their king. No trophy would cheer the Egyptians more than my head held aloft on a gleaming spear point. Disguise offered the best protection. In an ordinary battle chariot and in cavalryman's garb, I would attract the least attention and best be able to direct our strategy.

Not that I was afraid to die. Though not yet forty, I had already enjoyed a long and eventful reign. My reforms had literally changed the face of Judah's countryside. For more than twenty years I had been striving—and with marked success—to recover our past, to restore our ancient ways, to rebuild our citadel of faith.

My first opportunity to stem the tide of Assyrian corruption had come when I was about sixteen. The news of Ashurbanipal's death reached my palace. For four decades his restless troops had lived off the lands of his enemies. With a combination of ruthlessness and cunning he had held all rebels within and without his country in subjection to him. Now he was gone. As garments rip apart most readily at the seams, so kingdoms are most vulnerable at those points where the reign of one king is sewed to that of his successor. Often there is a struggle for the needle, and it takes months, even years, for the new king to stitch himself into place.

To an extent I succeeded in tearing Judah away. No king after Ashurbanipal had the power or the will to retaliate against my rebellion. Cautiously I began, changing what I could without bringing down on our heads vengeance from outside or dissent from inside. I began our reforms with the temple services and furnishings over which I and my nobles —remember I was just a young man—had direct control. The trappings of sun worship and astrology that Manasseh had installed were stripped away, and the worship of the Lord God of our fathers was reinstated.

A few years later, while the Assyrians were neck deep in trouble with the Scythians, two strong allies joined me in the battle for reform—the prophets Zephaniah and Jeremiah. Though they were less hopeful than I about what our reforms could achieve, they believed in what I was doing and helped the people understand why reform was needed and what shape it should take.

The two prophets, especially Jeremiah, knew that the corruption of the people was so deeply rooted in their hearts that it was as hard to get them to change their inner ways as for an Ethiopian to turn his skin white or for a leopard to erase his spots. Yet we had to try. My strong conviction was that the chief reason that God had allowed my father to be assassinated by his servants was that God wanted me to use all the power and wisdom he had given me to bring the people back to him. "Return" had been the call of the prophets to Judah's wandering sheep. As the shepherd of my people, I had to lead that return.

The greatest help that I received came entirely as a surprise. I have mentioned earlier the task of repairing the temple from the effect of my grandfather's wicked innovations. One day I sent my administrator, Shaphan, to the temple to count the money collected for the repairs and to pay the workmen. When he talked to Hilkiah the high priest about these matters, the priest brushed aside Shaphan's questions as though they were dust on the table.

Instead, in breathless sentences, Hilkiah told of an amazing discovery. In the course of the renovations he had come across the book of the law. Only after they had decided to inform me of the discovery did they settle the matter of the money owed to the workmen.

I found the words of the book utterly shattering. With torn garments and tear-stained cheeks I listened to line after line that Shaphan read.

Our situation in Judah was worse than I had dreamed. Worse in two ways: our idolatry and immorality were more flagrant than I knew; God's wrath against such acts was sharper than I imagined.

Huldah the prophetess confirmed my fears with blunt words: "Because they have forsaken me and have burned incense to other gods, that they might provoke me to anger with all the work of their hands, therefore my wrath will be kindled against this place, and it will not be quenched" (II Kings 22:17). With all my might I threw myself into the task of reform nationwide.

The elders and citizens, the priests and prophets, the women and children I gathered to Jerusalem to hear the words of God given through Moses his servant. As Joshua had done at Shechem twenty generations before, I put the choice to them as to which God they would serve. Then as far as possible I made that choice for them in solemn covenant with the Lord, and all the people joined me.

The results of the reform were astounding. Shrines were shattered on the hilltops. Images were smashed and burned. Idolatrous priests were thrown out of the high places where their pagan incense stank to the heavens. Shrine by shrine, altar by altar, idol by idol—my men went through the land and tore them down.

For days the smoke of the burning rubble at the brook Kidron and in the valley of the sons of Hinnom painted

Jerusalem with its ashes. My zeal for the worship of the Lord has known no bounds. All the resources of my throne have been put to his service.

And to guard those gains I ride to meet Necho. Where the true faith is at stake no price is too high, no cost too great.

Should Egypt's archers breach my armor, I shall go to my fathers in peace as Huldah said I would. And I shall go with the satisfaction that without reserve I spent myself for the true and living God. There can be no greater satisfaction than that.

Chapter 22

Zerubbabel:
Statesman Extraordinary

Now in the second year of their coming to the house of God at Jerusalem, in the second month, Zerubbabel the son of Shealtiel and Jeshua the son of Jozadak made a beginning, together with the rest of their brethren, the priests and the Levites and all who had come to Jerusalem from the captivity. They appointed the Levites, from twenty years old and upward, to have the oversight of the work of the house of the LORD. And Jeshua with his sons and his kinsmen, and Kadmiel and his sons, the sons of Judah, together took the oversight of the workmen in the house of God, along with the sons of Henadad and the Levites, their sons and kinsmen. And when the builders laid the foundation of the temple of the LORD, the priests in their vestments came forward with trumpets, and the Levites, the sons of Asaph, with cymbals, to praise the LORD, according to the directions of David king of Israel; and they sang responsively, praising and giving thanks to the LORD, "For he is good, for his steadfast love endures forever toward Israel." And all the people shouted with a great shout, when they praised the LORD, because the foundation of the house of the LORD was laid. (Ezra 3:8–11.)

It had to be the greatest passover since the days of Moses. Seven centuries and more had elapsed from the time our fathers and mothers sat to eat that first meal in Egypt. Staffs by their sides and sandals on their feet, they took that meal, ready to leave Egypt on a moment's notice. Confident that Pharaoh's plans would be confounded, believing that the Lord's plan to work their rescue would be effected, they ate in trembling and rejoicing. Protected by God's promise, shielded by blood on lintel and doorpost, they ate while death's own angel stalked the streets of Thebes and Memphis.

What a beginning our passover had! Moses's own words set its menu and declared its purpose. It bound us together in hope and expectation. It prepared us for our nationhood, as the meal that marked us as God's own people.

And now we were ready for another passover. Our eager anticipation had been building for months as we watched the roof take shape, the paneling applied, the gold inlaid. The temple of the Lord, the house of the living God, was about to be finished. Four hard years of toil, sweat, and sacrifice were drawing to a hopeful end—no, to a glorious beginning. The crowning feast would be the Lord's passover.

Its meal of lamb and herbs, of choice wine and unleavened bread would have for us a double meaning. The shadow of Egypt would hover over our tables, of course. We would remember the long years of slavery and the salvation of God's mighty arm. And we would relive that history with our children. Only a generation steeped in ingratitude could forget Moses, Aaron, Miriam, Joshua, Caleb, and all that generation whom God plucked up from the soil of bondage and carried toward the promised land.

But another shadow would cast its memories on the walls of our small homes this year. It was the shadow of exile in Babylon—seventy long years of it. Like our ancestors we had known the sting of a taskmaster's lash, the bite of an enemy's taunts, the loneliness of a captive's cot. Since the days when my grandfather Jehoiachin, Judah's last king, was taken in chains to the banks of the Euphrates, we had been unable to celebrate a proper passover. The Lord's song we had not sung in that strange land, or offered the Lord's sacrifices. David's strong city lay in ruins; Solomon's rich temple was a mound of rubble.

Now those chafing years of exile were past. The longing for Jerusalem had been answered. The temple had been rebuilt. Passover—the *Lord's* passover—was upon us. We could lift our songs, our *new* songs of praise, to God.

Our release came so rapidly that we were left breathless by its pace. It is true that Jeremiah told our grandparents that seventy years would be the length of our captivity. We should have known his words of hope would come to pass just like his words of doom. But it was hard to be hopeful in a land where ruthless kings held sway, where hollow myths were believed, where lifeless idols were revered.

Then it happened. As sudden as the dawn over the hills of Ammon, Cyrus appeared on the horizon of our history and brought brightness beyond believing to our dark days. From a minor Persian tribe he came, but within a few short years his name was on all of our lips.

Media was snatched away from its alliance with Babylon and joined to Cyrus's territory. Then Croesus, the powerful king of Lydia, felt the heel of Cyrus's boot. From the Persian mountains to the coasts of the Aegean, Cyrus was in control. Only Babylonia, shrunken in size and shriveled in power, stood in the way of his complete mastery of our part of the world.

In the course of a decade, Cyrus had Babylon at his feet—Nabonidus, her king, had surrendered and Belshazzar, her crown prince, was dead. Like a chaff-clearing breeze, Cyrus's rule brought fresh policies which left us wide-eyed with hope.

Nothing less than an entirely new way of governing peoples was his goal. Carefully he had studied the patterns of the empires of the past, and he sought to profit from their mistakes. The Assyrians, particularly, had earned endless amounts of ill will by their ruthless treatment of conquered peoples. They uprooted whole clans from their land and hurriedly planted them among people who did not share their language, culture, or religion. Worse still, the Assyrians imposed their own religions on their captives. The consequences of these harsh policies have been plain—rebellion and revolt wherever and whenever possible.

Cyrus set out to do differently. We could not help but feel that the hand of our God was leading him. Without knowing it, the great founder of the Persian empire had become a servant of Israel's Lord. Two edicts that Cyrus issued show how he was chosen to fit into God's purposes. One edict gave permission to return home to all of us Jews who were exiled in Cyrus's lands. "Thus says Cyrus king of Persia: The Lord, the God of heaven, has given me all the kingdoms of the earth, and he has charged me to build him a house at Jerusalem, which is in Judah. Whoever is among you of all his people, may his God be with him, and let him go up to Jerusalem, which is in Judah, and rebuild the house of the Lord, the God of Israel—he is the God who is in Jerusalem; and let each survivor, in whatever place he sojourns, be assisted by the men of his place with silver and gold, with goods and with beasts, besides freewill offerings for the house of God which is in Jerusalem" (Ezra 1:2-4).

The second edict went into even more detail about the size and construction of the temple. The fact that Cyrus put all this in writing and had it stored in the royal archives was of substantial help to us after his death, as I shall tell in a moment.

Who could have hoped for all that Cyrus promised? Who could fully believe it when it happened? We were free to go back to Judah. We were permitted to rebuild the temple. We were assured the resources to accomplish that deed. Our faith in the God of our fathers mounted to new heights. Even as I gaze at the walls and pillars of the great house of God, I marvel at the ways God used to bring it about.

Obstacle after obstacle he helped us overcome. One obstacle was the danger of compromise. No sooner had Joshua, the high priest, and I rallied the people to start building than some people came south to Jerusalem and offered to join us in our project. They professed even a desire to share in our worship. This we could not tolerate. The mixed nature of their worship was well known. Half-breeds these Samaritans were in culture, blood, and faith. The purity of our worship according to the laws of Moses would be in danger of pollution. We could not stand the thought that our dream of worship pure and free that had kept us alive in Babylon would now turn to vapor in Judah.

We paid dearly for our decision not to compromise. The Samaritans turned on us, and nipped at our heels like mean dogs for years on end. Their wrath reached its boiling point when they wrote the Persian governor to accuse us of sedition and revolution against his power. Their lies were believed by him, and he issued a decree which shut down our project. These foreigners, moved into our lands by the Assyrians, had succeeded in frustrating our plans and dampening our spirits almost as much as Nebuchadnezzar's army which had led away our fathers seventy years before.

Our people had no choice but to defer their dreams and give themselves to the tasks of reclaiming their lands and rebuilding their homes. For fifteen years the temple lay there —a bare foundation and a brass altar.

As the years rolled by, our own apathy became an obstacle as formidable as the Samaritan opposition. Repossessing our land became an all-consuming enterprise. Brick by brick we built our houses. Stone by stone we cleared our fields. Town by town we organized our governments, trying to keep the laws of the Medes and Persians, while remaining faithful to the customs of our fathers. And we did all this in a season of prolonged drought, where the threat of failing crops hung like a shroud over all of our activities. The sweat of our toil and the hurt of our hunger became much more real to us than the hope of a temple.

Then the Lord intervened. As suddenly as he had sent Cyrus as a servant to return us to Judah, so he sent prophets—two of them—to rekindle our will to build. What a personal impact they had on me, Haggai and Zechariah. Haggai wasted no words in telling us that our priorities were in disarray: "Is it a time for you yourselves to dwell in your paneled houses, while this house lies in ruins?" (Haggai 1:4). Another word of his struck an even stronger blow. Because we had postponed the completion of the temple, Haggai announced, God had withheld his blessings. Our famine was of our own making. Our apathy had bound God's hands.

What effect did the prophets' messages have? Well, just three weeks after the Lord spoke through Haggai, the crews were ready, the tools were at hand, and the building was resumed.

God had overcome our apathy. But other obstacles had

yet to be leveled. This time it was not the Samaritans but the Persian governor who objected, though we wondered whether the Samaritans had put him up to it. Rebellion was the last thing the governor and his associates wanted. The inspectors that Darius, the present king of Persia, sent around checked regularly on the peacefulness of each province. The eyes and ears of the king, these inspectors were called, and they roamed through the provinces from India to Ethiopia reporting to the king on the honesty, efficiency, and loyalty of each governor.

Tattenai, our governor, did not want to risk a bad report. When he tried to stop our project, we explained that Cyrus nearly twenty years before had granted his permission for our temple project. And more than that, we told Tattenai, Cyrus had provided funds for the building and had guaranteed the safe return of the sacred vessels—silver and gold—that Nebuchadnezzar's troops had carried to Babylon as booty of war.

We continued our labors, while we waited several weeks for Tattenai's messenger to return from Persia. Our joy burst all bounds, when we finally got the news. Darius's men had searched the royal archives and found Cyrus's original edict. What one Persian king had ordered, his successor had supported. Tattenai was in the clear, and our work sped ahead.

Perhaps our own discouragement proved to be the greatest obstacle after all. As the walls of the temple rose and its shape began to loom over the foundations that had been laid earlier, the hearts of many began to sink. Well we knew the glories of Solomon's splendid temple. Our parents had painted detailed pictures of the paneled walls, the bronze furnishings, the gold and silver decorations. Nothing we could build would match that former glory. We had neither the wealth nor the craftsmen of Solomon.

As political leader of Judah and representative to the Persian governor, I used all my influence to prod the people on. But the discouragement was too dark to be scattered by the candle of my influence. It took the bright light of God's word through Haggai to make the difference. God spoke to Joshua and me directly: "Yet now take courage, O Zerubbabel ... take courage, O Joshua ...take courage, all you people of the land...and I will fill this house with splendor.... The latter splendor of this house shall be greater than the former. . . ." (Haggai 2:4, 7, 9).

That word stretched our spirits to hope. And as we prepare the passover offerings, our hearts leap with that hope. Egypt we will remember, and our deliverance from slavery. Babylon we will recall, and our return from exile. But even more, our passover will ring with hope.

The God who moved the will of Cyrus, the God who confounded the plans of the Samaritans, the God who steadied the hand of Darius, the God who prompted the words of Haggai—that God is with us. And his best days for us are yet to come.

Chapter 23

Esther:
Queen for a Time of Crisis

Then Mordecai told them to return answer to Esther, "Think not that in the king's palace you will escape any more than all the other Jews. For if you keep silence at such a time as this, relief and deliverance will rise for the Jews from another quarter, but you and your father's house will perish. And who knows whether you have not come to the kingdom for such a time as this?"

Then Esther told them to reply to Mordecai, "Go, gather all the Jews to be found in Susa, and hold a fast on my behalf, and neither eat nor drink for three days, night or day. I and my maids will also fast as you do. Then I will go to the king, though it is against the law; and if I perish, I perish."

(Esther 4:13-16.)

It was an act of God's providence, nothing more and nothing less. In fact, it was the latest act in a whole drama of providence that had been played out before our very eyes.

Look at him, my cousin Mordecai—clad in royal robes, entrusted with the king's signet ring, bathed with the honor of the people. A few short months ago he was doomed to swing from the highest gallows ever seen in Susa, our capital. Now only Ahasuerus outranks him in all the Persian provinces—127 of them—that stretch from the valley of the Indus River in the east to the cataracts of the Nile in the west.

God's hand has provided Mordecai the power to rule firmly, and God's heart has granted him the insight to deal wisely with all the people—Jews and Gentiles alike. What a surprise it will be to the generations following when they browse through the royal records and find that a Jewish exile whose great-grandfather came to Babylon in chains with Nebuchadnezzar's troops was a leading figure in the Persian empire in the heyday of its power!

A surprise indeed to outsiders, but not to those who know our story. Unusual—of course it is—for Mordecai to find such prominence in a foreign court. Unusual, but not unprecedented. God's hand had worked such deeds before. Was it not God's plan that took Joseph from prison and placed him at Pharaoh's side? Was it not God's design that led the Egyptian princess to spy the basket with the baby Moses in it bobbing among the reeds? Was it not God's power that snatched Daniel from the lion's jaws and made him second only to the king?

God's providence—its power knows no limits; its grace has no measure. How lavishly it has been poured out in our midst during these last ten years or so! To recount the story is to verge on the incredible, unless we remember who our God is.

For me the proofs of God's providence began when I was selected among the virgins from whom the king would choose his next queen. Vashti, who had served at his side for years, had incurred his wrath—and in public at that. The occasion was one of the largest banquets that Susa's

palace had ever seen. From the fringes of the empire
Ahasuerus had invited his nobles and governors. The
satraps of each province, the commanders of the army and
navy, and the princes from every part of the realm were
on hand to view the splendor of the Persian court. It was
more than a display of wealth, this panorama which
lasted nearly half a year. It was also a demonstration of
power. The king had a message in mind as he summoned
the leadership to the splendors of his palace. That message
was plain: stand by me and share this wealth and glory;
turn against me and all this might well be used to crush
you.

The nobles and governors, the commanders and princes
got the message. They were staggered by the plush curtains
hung from silver rings, by the mosaics of marble and
mother-of-pearl, by the golden goblets and the royal wine.
But they were also sobered at the thought of the limitless
resources, the boundless power that such a king could command against them, should he choose. Early in his reign he
wanted to teach them who was in charge. It was a well-
taught lesson.

This was why Vashti's rebellion so inflamed him. With
the whole world at his beck and call, he could not get his
own wife to obey him. Not that I blame her. His request
had a taint of lewdness to it. To begin with, the king and
his friends were drunk. For seven days they had been at
it—with the wine flowing like the water in a Zagros mountain stream. The drink had put them in a bawdy mood.
They wanted entertainment—dancing, sensuous and wild.
Vashti's sense of dignity was offended. She was not about
to expose her charms to the evil stares, grasping clutches,
and crude jokes of drunken men. Wine is a great leveler,
and princes in their cups have no more manners than
drunken galley slaves.

Vashti's refusal to perform at the banquet sobered the
whole affair like the chill of icy water. It was Memucan,
one of the seven Persian princes, who summed up the
situation: "Not only to the king has Queen Vashti done
wrong, but also to all the princes and all the peoples who
are in all the provinces of King Ahasuerus. For this deed
of the queen will be made known to all women, causing
them to look with contempt upon their husbands. . . ."
(Esther 1:16–17).

So Vashti was deposed. And a contest to select a new

queen was begun. Throughout the provinces went the word calling for the loveliest maidens in the empire to be brought to the capital. I was chosen. An accident of beauty, it might be called. I prefer to view it as an act of providence.

Nervous as a young fawn running before the hounds, I left my cousin and guardian, Mordecai, and went to the royal harem. My edginess had two causes: the dread of displeasing the king, and the fear that my Jewish blood would be discovered. Throughout the whole year of preparation, while the oil and spices were enhancing my beauty, I hid like a treasure the secret of my origins.

Then the fateful night arrived. It was my turn to have my charms tested by the king. What could I do but seek to please him with my grace and my love. His pleasure was my one aim, during the short night given to me to prove myself a worthy queen. Somehow I was not as scared in his presence as I had been in the months of waiting. Deep down I sensed that my prayers—and those of Mordecai, who had sought my welfare daily—would see me through.

If I was surprised at my calmness, I was utterly stunned by the king's choice. What an awkward feeling it was to wear a crown and to adjust to the pomp and circumstance of royalty. Yet, as I look back, I see God's hand at work. More than Ahasuerus, it was he that steadied the crown on my head and seated me on the regal throne.

More than anything else it was a conversation with Mordecai that helped me understand this. There was nothing casual about that conversation. It took place in the midst of the sharpest crisis our Jewish people had known in years. The cause of the crisis was Haman the Agagite, who had wormed his way into a place of prominence and privilege with the king. Though he is long since dead, I have difficulty in mentioning his name without spitting it out between my teeth.

Haman and Mordecai had clashed from the beginning. With his keen perception, my old cousin had seen through Haman's wicked ambitions and refused to honor him as did the other elders of the city. Haman was livid with fury. Mordecai's integrity seemed to call Haman's attention to his own inner deceit, and, to cover that, he glowed with anger.

Even more, when he learned that Mordecai was Jewish, his furor was aimed at our whole race. His insecurity mounted to the point where he could not enjoy his power as long as one Jew remained to remind him of Mordecai's suspicions.

His anger boiled over into a murderous plot. Catching the king in a weak moment, Haman got him to sign an edict commanding the governors and the armies in all our provinces to exterminate my Jewish kinsmen. Even the way Haman chose to do this showed how wickedly superstitious he was. Day after day he cast lots until the right combination gave him the boldness to seek the king's cooperation in his fiendish plan.

This was the awful setting for my conversation with Mordecai, the conversation that burned in my mind the ways of God's providence as clearly as the handwriting on the wall in Daniel's day. There we were with the sentence of death hanging over us like a rock tottering above a mountain pass. The decree had been issued, the date set. The rock was poised to fall.

The conversation—I call it that, though it was actually a series of messages passed back and forth between Mordecai and me—slapped me awake. Mordecai wanted me to intercede with the king in behalf of our people. I told him that I could not go to see the king uninvited and that for thirty days the king had sent no call for me. Then it was that Mordecai opened my eyes to God's providence: "Think not that in the king's palace you will escape any more than all the other Jews. For if you keep silence at such a time as this, relief and deliverance will rise for the Jews from another quarter, but you and your father's house will perish. And who knows whether you have not come to the kingdom for such a time as this?" (Esther 4:13–14).

There was no arguing with Mordecai's words. That wisdom which had taught me so much of the ways of God and men found its target in my heart once again. Begging Mordecai and the other Jews in Susa to fast on my behalf, I determined to make our needs known to the king, even if it cost me my life.

How to approach the king was my question. As I prayed and pondered, a plan became clear. The hand of God was at work in my life. I began to see that it was he who had planted me in the court—and for one reason: to help rescue his people. His hand had been upon me for good even when I did not know it. If this was the hour for which he had brought me to the kingdom, he surely would not fail me now.

Nor would I fail him. Since Haman was the source of our suffering, I had to deal with him as well as the king. I invited them both to a banquet, where God gave me favor with my husband: "What is your petition?" he asked me when his heart was mellow with wine.

Haman gave me a dark look while he waited for my answer. He had been smitten by the events of the past days and seemed to quiver with rage like a trapped adder. His plan for vengeance on Mordecai had miscarried. He had fallen into his own trap.

Some years ago Mordecai had uncovered a plot against the life of Ahasuerus and had asked me to inform the king. The deed was duly noted in the royal chronicles, but no reward was tendered to Mordecai. Then the night before our banquet, when the king suffered a siege of restlessness, he recalled the episode and discovered that Mordecai had never been honored for his loyalty in saving the king's life.

The next day, the day of our banquet, he had asked Haman how he should honor a certain man. With his usual selfishness Haman assumed that he was the man. So he spelled out a lavish ritual of glory—royal robes, a prancing steed, a public parade with a crier heralding the man's great deeds. Then the blow fell. "Go do all that for Mordecai," the king commanded. The man Haman had wanted to hang he now had to honor.

No wonder he looked dark as the king put his question to me: "And what is your request? Even to the half of my kingdom, it shall be fulfilled" (Esther 7:2). Haman's dark look grew darker as I told the king of the devilish plot to destroy my people. The king's question was direct: "Who is he, and where is he, that would presume to do this?" (Esther 7:5). By now my courage had reached its summit. Straight in the eye I looked at Haman, my finger pointed at his sagging jaw. "A foe and enemy! This wicked Haman!" Slowly, forcefully, I measured the syllables.

The rest is history. Haman was hanged on the gallows he had built for Mordecai. My people in all the provinces were permitted to defend themselves on the day marked for their annihilation. God made the hearts of the enemy faint and the hands of our people strong. The king's law—part of the law of the Medes and Persians—could not be changed. But God caused him to issue another law, that the

Jews could resist their attackers. And resist they did in Persia, in Asia Minor, in Babylon, in Judah, in Egypt. Wherever we lived as God's scattered people, we felt his protecting arm.

Now Mordecai stands in a place of power. Our rights will be defended. As for me, I have the satisfaction of knowing that the God who gave Isaac to a barren Sarah, who graced the lips of Deborah with a song of victory, who prompted Jael to put Sisera to death, who led Bathsheba to establish Solomon on his throne was yet at work. He is God of our fathers—and our mothers. His mighty hand had used me—a humble Jewish woman— to bring deliverance to a multitude.

Chapter 24

Nehemiah:
Administrator with a Vision

Now I was cupbearer to the king. In the month of Nisan, in the twentieth year of King Artaxerxes, when wine was before him, I took up the wine and gave it to the king. Now I had not been sad in his presence. And the king said to me, "Why is your face sad, seeing you are not sick? This is nothing else but sadness of the heart." Then I was very much afraid. I said to the king, "Let the king live for ever! Why should not my face be sad, when the city, the place of my fathers' sepulchres, lies waste, and its gates have been destroyed by fire?" Then the king said to me, "For what do you make request?" So I prayed to the God of heaven. And I said to the king, "If it pleases the king, and if your servant has found favor in your sight, that you send me to Judah, to the city of my fathers' sepulchres, that I may rebuild it."

(Nehemiah 2:1–5.)

defined the city
secured defense
gave identity, security

That is it, I said to myself. Our work is complete. Our city has been restored. Our defense is secure. Our double defense, I should add, is secure.

Ezra's voice rang loudly above the standing throne as I carried on that conversation with myself. Section by section the wise scribe unrolled the scroll, and paragraph by paragraph we heard again the law of God.

So fresh it came to us, it was as though we stood again at Sinai's foot with Moses and the tablets. It was as though we joined with Josiah to hear the book of the law discovered in the temple.

To me the experience was particularly gratifying. Judah was not my home. Perhaps it would be better to say that I was not born there, because to every Jew Judah is home. I was born and raised in Persia. My family had decided not to return with Zerrubbabel and the others who left Babylon when Cyrus gave the exiles permission to return nearly a century ago.

The Persian court where I had been raised and where I had served as cupbearer to the king was a world away from Jerusalem's dry hills and crude houses. Yet Jerusalem held a fascination for me that outshone the splendor of all three Persian capitals—Ecbatana to the north, Persepolis to the south, and Susa in between. Summer palace and winter palace, the Persian kings had them both, and they were adorned with all the art and ornamentation that the Persian coffers could afford. But they were not Jerusalem.

David had not built his home in them. Solomon had not constructed his temple there. Those magnificent Persian cities—and I had seen them all as I traveled at the king's side—did not shelter the ark of God's presence; their courts were not hallowed with the memory of a hundred passovers; their walls had not rung with the music of a thousand psalms. Part of me was always in Jerusalem, though I never saw its towers until I was a grown man.

Now I was there, listening to Ezra read the law, watching the sun caress the new walls with its dancing rays. The law and the walls—what a combination they were. The defense of Jerusalem, of Judah, of God's program to bring salvation to his people, was up to them. Would they be adequate? Others may have raised that question, but I had no doubt. Thoughts of God's ways—the sheer wonder of them—swarmed in my heart like bees around a hive.

I recalled the sadness that darkened my spirit when I first heard of Jerusalem's desolation. I was at Susa serving in the king's court, supervising the royal household and attending the personal needs of the king as one of his most trusted officers. There came to the court a relative of mine named Hanani. He and some associates had just made the lengthy journey from Jerusalem, and their news of the city was up to date. But it was also grim: "The survivors there in the province who escaped exile are in great trouble and shame; the wall of Jerusalem is broken down, and its gates are destroyed by fire" (Nehemiah 1:3).

"The Samaritans?" I asked. And their quiet nods confirmed my suspicions. During the days when Zerubbabel was governor of the province Beyond the River, as we called Judah and the territory surrounding it, the Samaritans had done all they could to block the rebuilding of the temple. Now, more recently, they had annoyed the people of Judah by thwarting their attempts to put Jerusalem in order. Sections of the city wall they had toppled, and the tall wooden gates they had burned.

The Persian officials had turned their backs on this mayhem. The memories of revolt in Egypt were fresh on their minds. Any walled city they viewed as a threat. So if the Samaritans wanted to harass Jerusalem, they were free to do so. At least the Jews could not mount a rebellion against Persian power. Not from a demoralized, unprotected capital!

No news in my lifetime had so shattered me. For days I wept and mourned, as though my family had been felled by a plague. Fasting and praying were my daily occupation. Only one human being had power to bring healing to Jerusalem's sores, and that was Artaxerxes, the king whom I served. Day and night my prayer was that the God who keeps covenant with those who love him would move the king's heart to intervene on our behalf.

Then it happened in a way I did not plan. The king detected my sadness, which I had always tried to mask in his presence, and asked me about it. What could I do but tell him the truth and pray that God would use that conversation for good? "Let the king live forever," I exclaimed, bowing before him. "Why should not my face be sad, when the city, the place of my fathers' sepulchers, lies waste, and its gates have been destroyed by fire?" (Nehemiah 2:3).

The rest of the conversation went more smoothly than I could have dreamed. The king granted me a leave from his service and gave me authority to go to Judah to supervise the restoration of Jerusalem. I was to carry a letter to Asaph, the keeper of the royal forest in Lebanon, giving permission to use timber for the various building projects, especially the city gates. The God of wonders was at work. Like a gazelle his power had overleaped the first great obstacle: Artaxerxes had offered full cooperation.

But a much greater barrier greeted me when I arrived in the province Beyond the River. The Samaritans were not inclined to take my project lying down. With incredible energy and unbelievable resourcefulness they set about blocking our plan. And they had a great deal of help from some of Judah's neighbors, like the Ammonites east of Jordan. During the exile all these people had enjoyed access to our land. The Jews who had stayed home were too few, too old, and too weak to protect our boundaries.

Our neighbors—if that is the right word for them—pastured their flocks in our fields, watered them at our wells, and sheltered them in our folds. Their opposition to the rebuilding of our state was no surprise, therefore. The Samaritans did not fully share our law, our faith, our customs—mixed race that they were, born of a combination of Israelite stock and foreign blood brought to Samaria by the Assyrians more than two hundred years ago. As for the Ammonites and others, they had almost always been enemies of ours since David's time, when they became vassal states obligated to serve the kings of Judah. Some of our neighbors—Edom, for instance—had even joined in the looting of Jerusalem during Nebuchadnezzar's siege. Worse still, they had captured some of our refugees and sold them into slavery.

All of this helps to account for the fiendish opposition that we faced when the rebuilding began. It was an opposition as varied as it was devilish. At first they tried to dishearten us by taunting and mocking: "Yes, what they are building—if a fox goes up on it he will break down their stone wall!" Such was the jeer of Tobiah the Ammonite (Nehemiah 4:3). But the work went on, as family by family and town by town the men worked at sections of *familirs together*

the wall. Divide and conquer was my motto. And I cut the task into pieces that each group could handle.

What a joy it was to see the enterprise finally under way —rubble being cleared, stones being quarried, timber being shaped. From all over Judah came our countrymen, responsive to my call, submissive to my authority.

But the enemies persisted. If their insults were a nuisance, their attacks became a menace. Led by Sanballat, a Samaritan whose cunning was matched by his viciousness, they threatened force against us. We had to change our tactics, posting half our people as guards and half as workers. Many was the time that I toiled beside my men with a trowel in one hand and a sword in the other. We even took to sleeping in the city rather than returning to the villages where we lived, so eager were we to protect our work.

Block upon block the wall rose as our craftsmen kept one eye on the plumb line and the other on our foe. As the breaks in the wall were all sealed and the towers pushed toward their full height, Sanballat and his allies tried one more ploy: they sought to destroy my leadership by getting me to compromise. They offered to consult with me. I refused, both because I was too busy and because my countrymen would interpret any consultation as fear. The trust in God which I had encouraged and exemplified would be betrayed, confidence in me would be broken, and our morale would shatter like an eggshell.

52   It is hard to believe that in just fifty-two days we accomplished our task, despite the goading of the Samaritans. God had shown himself to be for us, and his work prospered in our hands.

Wild animals would no longer stalk our streets at night. Brigands would no longer break in and steal. The citizens of Jerusalem who had sought shelter with relatives in other towns could now sleep safely in their own homes. Our enemies would no more taunt us and ask "Where is your God that he cannot protect his city?" Jerusalem is secure.

But it took more than walls to do it. It also took God's law as a reminder of our covenant privileges and obligations. If there was cooperation in the building of the wall, there was division over the distribution of wealth. Taxation was high; the income of the farmers and workers was low. We faced a kind of revolution. People were incensed at the poverty, forced as they were to borrow money to pay taxes and buy food. What stung the poor people most keenly was the fact that Jews were oppressing their fellow Jews with high prices and outlandish interest rates.

As governor, duly appointed by the Persian king, I had to do something about the crisis. Even more, as a servant of God's commandments I had to see that justice was done. I used the full weight of my office and whatever persuasive powers I had to insist that the wealthy lower the prices, lend money without interest, and return land that had been snatched away through foreclosure proceedings.

Walls were not enough, though God had helped us build them. Righteousness was the only real defense on which God's people could count.

I listened to Ezra read the blessings and cursings of the law—the reward and the punishment with which God weighed our loyalty or disloyalty to his ways. As I listened I looked at Jerusalem's strong tower; I followed the march of her walls from section to section; I eyed the massive planks of cedar, strapped into gates with copper bands. The double defense: a wall to ward off enemies without, a law to control the enemies within us.

As I listened and as I looked, I prayed: Lord, keep both defenses strong for the sake of your holy name. *yes*

double defense:
wall — outer
law — inner

Cf. America:
defense - yes
but what about morality?

Chapter 25

Ezra:
Teacher of the Law of God

While Ezra prayed and made confession, weeping and casting himself down before the house of God, a very great assembly of men, women and children, gathered to him out of Israel; for the people wept bitterly. And Shecaniah the son of Jehiel, of the sons of Elam, addressed Ezra: "We have broken faith with our God and have married foreign women from the peoples of the lands, but even now there is hope for Israel in spite of this. Therefore let us make a covenant with our God to put away all these wives and their children, according to the counsel of my lord and of those who tremble at the commandment of our God; and let it be done according to the law. Arise, for it is your task, and we are with you; be strong and do it." Then Ezra arose and made the leading priests and Levites and all Israel take oath that they would do as had been said. So they took the oath.

(Ezra 10:1–5.)

One by one they filed by. I watched them through tear-clouded eyes. Nehemiah, the governor, led the way. Behind him stood the priests like Zedekiah, Seraiah, and Azariah. After the priests came the Levites, dedicated servants of the temple, men who prepared the sacrifices, cared for the vessels, directed the music—men like Jeshua, Binnui, Kadmiel, and Malluch.

Each of them with their fellow priests and Levites paused for a moment at the table which held the document. Soberly they scanned its contents; gently they poured a spot of wax on it, and firmly they stamped the wax with their signet rings. The document was thus solemnized by the personal pledges of our most distinguished religious leaders.

For me it was a dream come true. My people were pledging themselves in holy covenant to walk in the ways of our God, the God whom our Persian rulers called the God of heaven, the God whom we knew as the God of Abraham, Isaac and Jacob.

Think how I felt in those difficult years in Babylonia. All my life I had thought of Judah as our spiritual home. Its towns and villages, its rugged hills and gentle valleys I had never seen. Jerusalem was a word I had heard every day of my life, but I had never walked its streets or bargained in its market. Yet those places—Judah and Jerusalem—were the center of our living, the anchor of our destiny.

That was why the reports had hurt so—the reports of a faith that was in neglect, a tradition that was being ignored, a law that was virtually abandoned. When opportunity came to do something about those reports, I seized it with both hands. With the backing of the Persian court—Artaxerxes was king—I formed an expedition and set out for Judah. With me were some members of my own family of priests, who like me traced their ancestry back to Aaron, the great high priest who was also brother to Moses to whom God first gave our law. Other members of Levi's tribe accompanied us. Their families had been the singers, gatekeepers, and servants in the temple before Nebuchadnezzar's rough troops dragged our forefathers off to Babylon in chains.

With those of us who were religious leaders came a host of our fellow Israelites, representing some of our finest clans. What a mountain of supplies we had to pile up for the journey! Almost two thousand men and their families, we set out on a journey that would take about four months. Bag and baggage, we set out. This was no holiday visit. It was a permanent migration. We were going home. After over a century of exile, after generations of living in a foreign land, we were going home.

More than our baggage and supplies we carried with us. For one thing, we had a letter from Artaxerxes, the Persian king. In great detail it spelled out the nature of our mission and the king's support of it. It rang with a generosity that reminded us of what Cyrus had done for Zerubbabel decades earlier: "I make a decree," Artaxerxes had written, "that any one of the people of Israel or their priests or Levites in my kingdom, who freely offers to go to Jerusalem, may go with you. . . . The vessels that have been given you for the service of the house of your God, you shall deliver before the God of Jerusalem. And whatever else is required for the house of your God, which you have occasion to provide, you may provide it out of the king's treasury. . . . And you, Ezra," the king's edict went on to conclude, ". . . appoint magistrates and judges who may judge all the people in the province Beyond the River. . . . Whoever will not obey the law of your God and the law of the king, let judgment be strictly executed upon him. . . ." (Ezra 7:13, 19–20, 25–26).

The Aramaic words leaped at me from the page when I first read them. There they were, the permission, the approval, the sponsorship of the king. All that I had prayed for—and more. My heart burst with praise: "Blessed be the Lord, the God of our fathers, who put such a thing as this into the heart of the king, to beautify the house of the Lord which is in Jerusalem, and who extended to me his steadfast love before the king and his counselors, and before all the king's mighty officers" (Ezra 7:27–28).

We proudly carried the king's document with us. Another part of our luggage was silver and gold from the Persian treasuries—a royal gift to help us beautify the temple which the Babylonian troops had so thoroughly stripped and which Zerubbabel and Haggai had only partially rededicated. I thrilled to think that part of Haggai's bright prophecy was being fulfilled through our venture: "and I will shake all nations," was what God had promised, "so that the treasures of all nations shall come in, and I will fill this house with splendor. . . ." (Haggai 2:7).

The king's document and the king's wealth—what precious cargo! But some things even more precious we carried with us. In fact, I scarcely let them out of my sight the entire four months. Had we been attacked by marauders along the way—which, thanks to God, we were not—I would have given my life to protect them. The scrolls of the law of Moses were our most prized possessions. I thought of them as I watched the priests and Levites file by. I thought of the law as I heard each signet ring stamp its seal of endorsement on the covenant. What they were pledging to do—that long line of priests and Levites— was to make that law their guide to life.

Nothing could have pleased me more. I was a scribe by birth and training. Caring for the scrolls of the law, teaching the law, interpreting the law, were my calling. That was one reason why I found Babylonia so frustrating. Much of the law could not be kept without the temple and its altars. Furthermore, our law was so comprehensive, so all-inclusive, so totally binding, that it had to have the full support of civil law to make it work. Take the sabbath, as an instance. Halting work, stopping all trade, enforcing rest on a community could not be done by religious officials alone. The entire government had to cooperate. Yet in Babylonia this could not happen. We Jews were a small minority in a teeming multitude of persons who feared not our God, knew not our traditions, kept not our sabbath. We did the best we could to keep our own identity, but we, especially our young people, were always in danger of being devoured and digested by the pagan culture around us.

For that reason, when I saw Nehemiah stamp his sign on the covenant scroll I could not keep from shouting hallelujah. He was the governor. Nehemiah had been appointed by Artaxerxes to represent him in our satrapy or province which the Persians called "Beyond the River."

We had made a good team, Nehemiah and I. We had built Jerusalem's double defense: the wall and the law. Artaxerxes had given us authority to use his power to enforce the law of Moses. That was part of the decree we carried with us. And Nehemiah was used of God to back that decree to the letter.

How remarkable are the paths of providence! A royal cupbearer named Nehemiah was so burdened for the

welfare of Jerusalem that his king sent him west to look to
the needs of the city. Meanwhile, a scribe named Ezra
who lived in Babylon, not Persia, was being prepared by
God to cooperate with Nehemiah in reorganizing the life
of God's people around the law.

Who but God could have prompted me to collect, study,
and edit the stories and laws which our fathers have
treasured since the days of Moses. Every manuscript or
scroll I could get my hands on I pored over until the oil
in my clay lamp burned low. Every elder and priest who
had known well the laws and customs of our people I questioned with keen intensity, making notes on parchment
with my iron pen. Day after day I spent arranging the
records of our past from those seven days of Genesis that
set the world moving, through the promises of God to
Abraham and his offspring, to the death of Moses on
Nebo's bald summit. And everything in between I copied
from our treasured documents that had been smuggled with
us to Babylon in the dark night of our captivity: the account of our exodus from Egypt and our encounter with
God at Sinai—and all the laws, especially the laws. Babylon made them unspeakably precious to us.

They were the marks of our difference—those laws. We
did not become different from other people because we
kept them. We kept them because we were different. God
had called Abraham to father a nation; God had called
Moses to lead that nation into statehood in a new land.
That history was what made us different. And our law was
the way we expressed our difference in every aspect of
our life. Stamp, stamp, stamp went the seals. Quiet, yet
solid, testimonies those stamps were of our pledge to be
God's unique people—and to keep his law flying at full
staff before us, the banner of our uniqueness.

I had carried that law to Judah with the tenderness
reserved for a first-born child. But putting it into practice
required strength along with tenderness. The rumors that
were wafted to Babylon like feathers in the desert breeze
proved to be more true than I had feared: the people of
Judah, including the leadership, had badly compromised
with the religions and customs of our neighbors. The chief
way that they had done this might seem innocent at first:
they had taken wives from among the peoples who worshiped other gods—Hittites, Jebusites, and Canaanites who
lived in our land, particularly around Jerusalem; Am-

monites and Moabites, our distant cousins, who lived east of Jordan and the Dead Sea; Egyptians, from whose hands God had once for all delivered us.

Lest I be misunderstood, it was not just the mixing of blood that raised the terrible problem. It was the mixing of cultures. The strange ways were built into the lives of those women like the marrow of their bones. The worship of their idols was an unchangeable part of their practice. I was ashamed to note that the faith of the men of Judah was often swamped like a tiny boat in a Galilean storm by the religion of their wives. Children were caught between two faiths and left with confusion and doubt.

Had we come all the way from Babylon to see God's purposes defeated by mixed marriage? Had we escaped the contamination of the religions of Marduk and Zoroaster to succumb to the myths of Baal, Chemosh, and Dagon?

Nothing but the law could remedy the situation. Matters looked quite settled as I watched Nehemiah and the priests pledge their loyalty to the God who gave his law to Moses. But they did not look that way when I first built that wooden pulpit and stood to read the law. Would anybody listen? Would my reading foment a revolt? Would the leaders grab me by force and drop me in a dungeon as they had done to Jeremiah a century and a half before?

None of my fears came to pass. Instead, and I marveled at it, the people wept. The reading of the law stirred old and hidden chords—chords of memory, chords of devotion, chords of gratitude, chords of repentance. Those chords, strummed by the law of Moses, changed all of Judah's music. I could hear the difference with my own ears.

Wives were sent back to their families, with tears of course, but also with the awareness that the continuation of our national life depended on the purity of our faith. We were either God's people or no people. Whatever it took to assure our loyalty to him had to be done.

So I watched the solemn file of leaders. I heard the gentle stamp of the signet rings, I looked at the seals set in the firming wax, and I rejoiced.

The law of God which had been my sacred trust had done its work. The God of the law had again conquered the hearts of his chosen people.

Conclusion

These, then, are the stories of some of the people God used. Strange heroes they are! The most important thing about them is that they knew God. And the record of their experiences in the Bible is one of the ways in which God introduces himself to us.

Their lives, from Abraham to Ezra, span a millennium and a half of forward movement in God's program to make himself heard to an unheeding world. A whole library of revelation is found in their biographies—volume after volume unrolling the wonders of God's works. Seized by God's Spirit, these two dozen and more men and women played vital parts in God's program.

They teach us lessons of many kinds: their lives are examples of failure and trust, of obedience and success. Most of all they bring us lessons about the God of the Bible, the only true and living God. Their experiences remind us that he gets his will done despite the severe limitations of the people through whom he works. Their stories instruct us how God uses persons like us as part of his accommodation to human weakness. Their pilgrimages inform us that God has both the power to override obstacles of history and the love to make that history serve his high purposes.

The special role these people played in God's plan of redemption and in his inspired Scriptures makes them unique. The Bible will not be expanded to include our stories along with theirs.

But God has not stopped working. And persons open to his love and grace are still what he uses. Not just people tall and great, not just people bold and brave, not just people wise and learned. But all kinds of people. Strange heroes. People like Deborah and Hannah, like Ruth and Solomon, like Josiah and Zerubbabel—like you and me.